Tales From The Clay Country

WORKING WITH STEAM IN CORNWALL

Working with steam in Cornwall. Small prairie 4563 stands in the loop at Gwinear Road with the 2.25pm to Helston on 30 May 1960. While waiting for the main line service the fireman takes the opportunity to 'trim' the bunker – breaking up some of the larger coal lumps. L.R. Freeman, www.transporttreasury.co.uk

PHILIP E. RUNDLE M.B.E., M.Inst. T.A.

Irwell Press Ltd.

DEDICATION

For Gerald and James, who have both not only become a very valuable part of my family, but have given me support which I know I can rely upon.

Also for Violet (Vi) Giles and Les Haines, both of whom contributed to this work but sadly have since died.

For the men, too, who worked upon the steam locomotives of the West Country; may their fires never burn dull, nor may they want for that extra pound of steam.

And for Railwaymen everywhere, whatever their designation or loyalty – that this small token might be accepted as a tribute to their professionalism and service.

ACKNOWLEDGEMENTS

A difficulty which I have experienced as a new author is how to arrange this most important part of the book. It would be easy to use almost as many pages as there are in the text, and still end up with someone left out.

I have largely acknowledged reminiscences as and where they appear in the text, but a mention must be made of the many railwaymen, the wives and offspring of railwaymen now sadly passed on, and the many others who have written to me since the publication of *Laira Fireman*, to whom I have replied personally.

I heartily thank the many photographers whose work brings the written word to life, in particular Terry Nicholls and I am most grateful to the Transport Treasury for making available images from their comprehensive collection. Locally Chris Horsham was instrumental in obtaining the work of Roy Parkes, and no book telling the story of railways would be complete without efforts from Maurice Dart. I also owe a debt of gratitude to Steve Jenkins, Librarian of the Cornwall Local Studies Library at Redruth for his most generous help. Also Sarah Lloyd-Durrant, Curator, Royal institution of Cornwall and Royal Cornwall Museum, for invaluable assistance.

As ever, I pay tribute to my Wife, Joyce, for her patience and understanding, while the computer keyboard clicked away merrily (and at times not so). My daughter, Sue, has ever been 'at hand' to settle me down when things went wrong, and once again I have to thank granddaughter Philippa for correcting my punctuation etc. Education is a wonderful thing!

In my adopted home town of Saltash we have a bookshop called *The Bookshelf*, a gem of a place, a fountain of information, and not only about books. I owe an immense debt to the 'Lady of the Shop', one Jill Male, whose support knows no bounds and whose enthusiasm seems without limits.

I cannot find the words to thank my publishers, Irwell Press. They did me proud with my first book, and I have every confidence that this one will be of the same very high standard.
Philip E. Rundle M.B.E.
Saltash, 2011

First published in the United Kingdom in 2011
by Irwell Press Limited, 59A, High Street, Clophill,
Bedfordshire MK45 4BE
Printed by Shortrun Press, Exeter

Contents

14XX 0-4-2T 1419 taking water at Lostwithiel on 31 May 1960 after arrival with the 5.35pm auto train from Fowey. L.R. Freeman, www.transporttreasury.co.uk

Clay Country. Small prairie 4565 with a train of clay wagons, ex-Coombe Junction and characteristically tarpaulined to mitigate the effects of the stuff blowing everywhere along the route. The train is drawing into the yard at Liskeard, 31 May 1950. L.R. Freeman, www.transporttreasury.co.uk

Introduction

Following the interest shown in my first book, *Laira Fireman*, it was put to me that a second might be of interest, broadening the scope across Cornwall, a county so dear to my heart. In *Tales from the Clay Country*, I have attempted to portray the work of the Great Western in Cornwall and in particular the steam sheds at St Blazey, Truro and Penzance. After a while it seemed natural to include the Southern men and their engines at Wadebridge, on the North Cornwall line, to make this an account of *Cornish Sheds*. Yet, so intimately connected were the Western workings, there are inevitably more memories of the great shed at Laira, Plymouth which, however you look at it, remains stubbornly part of Devon. By attending the meetings of the Retired Sections of the Great Western Railway Staff Associations at Laira, St Blazey, St Austell, Truro and Redruth I have been able to glean snippets of the workings of those sheds. Sadly, a fact of life is that the 'Men of the Footplate', from the Steam Age are a diminishing breed, and this has made research that much more difficult. I pay tribute to the welcome which was extended to me at those meetings and to the resulting contributions towards the preparation of this book.

The Great Western main line from Plymouth down through the heart of Cornwall was almost like an artery, and was considered to be just as important to the way of life and the economy of the Duchy. The North Cornwall, in a smaller way, played the same vital role in the north of the county. The industries of mining and quarrying (tin, copper, clay in the south, clay and slate in the north), agriculture, horticulture and fishing, provided employment for the great part of the population. The railway played an important role in the growth of these same industries, opening up new markets countrywide and providing the vital transport to the dockside to send the fruits of their labours worldwide. As the demand for tin and copper slumped in the period after the First World War, the railway provided special trains for the Cornish miners, and in some cases their families too, to emigrate to the mining grounds of South Africa and America. My grandfather was one of those miners.

Over the years all of the above industries have declined, some to nothing and some to but a museum-piece shadow of their heyday. But as always seems to happen a new industry has developed, tourism. Much of the horticulture and some of the china clay working remains. Clay still goes by rail but with the road bridge at Saltash much of it is now taken by road. The days are long gone when, in a single season, over 250 special trains with cattle wagons laden with Cornish broccoli would depart by rail. A report in a local newspaper as early as 1868 stated that new potatoes despatched that year from Penzance amounted to some 3,000 tons. The same report gave the additional information that no less than six tons of butter left the station in a single day, destined for diverse parts of the country. Some 6,000 rail tankers of milk, and vans full to overflowing with flowers and fish all travelled by the rails. The records show that in 1945 nearly 140,000 tons of clay (something like 9,000 wagons) went by rail, and a similar amount by sea. That part which was carried to the various ports by rail, reached their destinations, in no small respect, through the efforts of the men who worked on the locomotives of the Great Western Railway. The sad fact is that a steep decline in demand for Cornish produce came in the 1960s – at the same time as the demise of the steam locomotive, which had served the clay so well.

For a short period in my working life I was a part of that special band of men, on the footplate, but circumstances decreed that I should leave the railway to find a career elsewhere. The memory of life on the footplate with all of the magical connotations of boyhood, has very much stayed with me, and I am grateful for the chance to document more of these stories, and especially those tales told to me by my former colleagues from the engine sheds at Laira, St Blazey, Truro, Penzance and Wadebridge.

For over a century and a half the railway has served the West Country, and for one hundred or so years steam bore the load. The employees of the Great Western Railway were known as 'Company Servants', and were proud to be designated as such; nowhere more so than on the footplate. This then is mostly *their* story, and I trust that you will enjoy their experiences as much as I have.

4585 at Bodmin General station 19 August 1958. A.E. Bennett, www.transporttreasury.co.uk

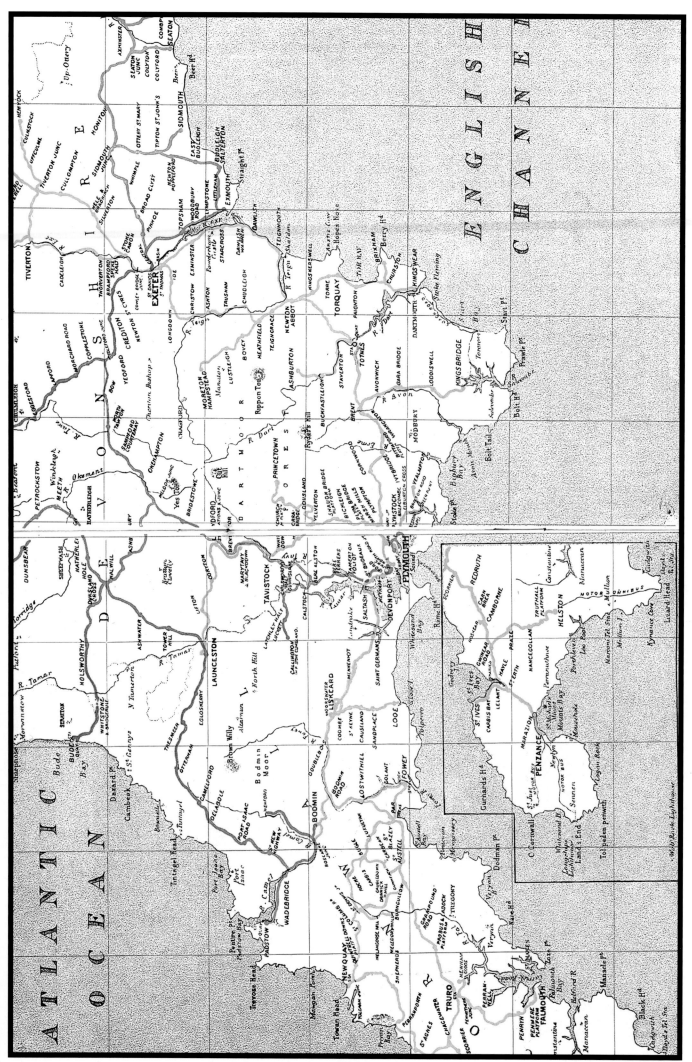

Chapter 1
On the Footplate

The normal relationship between an engine driver and his fireman was one of 'professional' understanding. The driver, of course was the man in charge, and to a working degree, his word was accepted as being The Law. Even so, there was a mutual respect which came from both accepting that the other was competent in doing his job. After all, regular pairings could last for five years or more until one or the other was promoted out of the link. Occasionally there were exceptions, as personalities were not always compatible and conflict, even fisticuffs on occasion, did occur. At times firemen on spare turns could be rostered with a different driver for a week, and this could sometimes create a difficulty as both had been used to working with their own 'mate', and had got used to each other's methods.

I was fortunate in my regular drivers and even when on a spare turn I can only recall one occasion when a driver was not keen to accept me. In this particular case the reason given was that the work belonged to the No.2 Passenger Link and I was a mere junior fireman, only recently promoted to the No.2 Goods Link – the first 'true' main line link at Laira. My

driver was duly overruled and, muttering, he took us off shed. I managed to put up enough of a show on the outward journey to Penzance and coped reasonably enough. His attitude had altered completely by the return to Plymouth and I even extracted some crumbs of backhanded praise – he solemnly informed the Newton Abbot crew who relieved us at North Road that though I was 'only a inexperienced fireman for the day', I wasn't, astonishingly, too bad.

My brother tells of an unusual set of circumstances with one of his drivers, a gentleman called Horace Carlyle. Horace had started his railway career at St Blazey engine shed a couple of years after the end of the First World War. As with all footplatemen, he was firstly a cleaner boy and eventually, as seniority and vacancies occurred, was promoted to fireman at Laira shed at Plymouth. In those days, on promotion, you were obliged to take up the next vacancy, wherever it might be. Horace was wrenched from his Cornish home to the new world of metropolitan Plymouth but he was lucky. He could have gone anywhere – Swansea, Wolverhampton or London where they couldn't understand you, nor you them!

Fireman Bill Rundle and Driver Harry Roach of Laira shed. This pairing in the Goods Link lasted for over five years, and developed into a lifetime of friendship even after Harry moved to live in Australia with his son and family. W.L. Rundle.

Below. Paddington station during the War years. A staged photograph to highlight the way women were taking over so many male jobs. The crew of the King 4-6-0 are Driver Bob Wheatley and Fireman Horace Carlyle of Laira shed, a long way from home. Note the tarpaulin and the plate fixed over the cab window, to hide the fire glow from enemy aircraft at night. The ladies are holding placards to indicate each job; nearest is a VAN GUARD, next to her a DINING CAR ATTENDANT. The lady far right is an ENGINE CLEANER.

Laira Junction on 16 July 1953; auto-fitted 0-6-0PT 6416 has a three coach (normal stock) branch train for Tavistock. It was on just such a train that the schoolboy Peter Williams at Bickleigh showed such interest in the engine! E.R. Morten.

Horace progressed through all the links, from working in the shunting yards and shed duties, known as the Pilot Link, to eventually reach the 'Top Link' at Laira where the work included 'double home' turns to London in which you lodged overnight in a 'barracks' provided by the railway or, more congenially (in theory) in a spare room of a railway widow. By now he had 'passed' for driver.

It was at this time, during the Second World War, that Horace was paired with a driver called Bob Wheatley, who was renowned as an excellent engineman. I am given to understand that all firemen who had worked with him had benefited greatly from the experience. Bob had one special trick. The cylinder lubricator on the footplate was placed in front of the driving position; it had a chamber containing a special heavy grade of oil and four sight glasses whereby the flow of oil could be observed and, if necessary, adjusted. Bob always placed an empty cigarette packet, broken open and with the white inside showing, behind those sight feeds so that the droplets of oil could more easily be seen. In after years, as a driver in his own right, Horace was to do the same. Should anyone ever write *Unlikely Things To Do With A Fag Packet* it would up there with the silver cups we used to make from the foil.

While with Bob Wheatley, Horace recalled being involved in a wartime 'propaganda' photo session to portray the role of women in the war effort. Having taken an engine from Old Oak Common shed to Paddington for a return passenger

train to Plymouth, they had to pose for the photographers with their locomotive standing in the platform road. On the platform was a line of twenty-one ladies dressed in all manner of railway uniform waving placards denoting the grades of work of the men they were replacing, who had been called-up into the Forces and had gone to war.

After my first book *Laira Fireman* had been published, I paid a visit to the retired members meeting at the Great Western Railway Staff Association (GWRSA) Social Club at Laira and was approached by Bob Thomas a former fireman and driver at Laira shed. Bob was indeed the son of Frank Thomas who did such sterling work as Laira's Member on the 'Central Council', a representative staff body elected by local footplatemen. Bob had read the book, and realised that when he too had been 'made' fireman for Slough engine shed, he had actually replaced me when I was posted back to Laira from Slough. Moreover he had actually been paired with my former driver 'Dai'. He had lodged in the same hostel as me and, of course, this then led to a host of reminiscences and shared memories, in which the nurses from the adjoining hospital seemed to feature to an inordinate degree. They always seemed so vibrant, whether going on or off duty; along with a waft of sweet scent, their chatterings and girlish giggles lingered in the air as they walked past. This was not at all like us who, dusty and sweaty after a shift, just wanted to 'drag' ourselves to our beds.

To pile coincidence upon coincidence, there then came a telephone call from a gentleman called Peter Williams. Having heard the publicity for my book on the TV and the wireless, he wanted to know whether I had worked on the Tavistock/Launceston branch. Assuredly that was so, and he then enquired about the early morning 'school train' to Tavistock. Did I recall a schoolboy getting on to the train at Bickleigh station? I was able to tell him that the train was the 7.40am from Plymouth North Road, arriving Bickleigh at somewhere about 8.00am. But was there anything *in particular* that I recalled? It suddenly dawned upon me that my driver Claude Bolt had indeed noticed a certain young schoolboy showing a keen interest in the locomotive; the lad had an infirmity (as did many more children then, due to now-vanished childhood diseases like polio) which affected his walking. I recalled Claude inviting him to ride in the cab on a couple of occasions, completely illegally, of course. Peter confirmed that this was indeed himself and, in fact, other drivers had also let him up on the footplate. The old adage stands true; it really is a small world and indeed Peter now lives just outside Saltash.

At the beginning of my career at Laira as a cleaner boy, I lived on the Cornish side of the River Tamar with my parents in Saltash; my meagre earnings ruled out even the thought of payment for lodgings. Now the train service was such that it was impossible to get to Laira shed for the early morning engine cleaning turn at 6 am. I explained my problem to Tom

Saltash station, 4 June 1960. The fireman of the 'motor' on arrival from Plymouth is concerned with replenishing the water tanks of his engine, 6421. Normal practice was to fill up every other journey. With the two 'cars' on the front care had to be taken not to allow excess water to splash over the departing passengers. James Harrold, www.transporttreasury.co.uk

Water taken on board, the empty train moved to the west cross-over, a short distance past the station and out on the Coombe viaduct, to return to the 'up' platform to load for the journey back to Plymouth. It was in similar circumstances, in the early days of my engine cleaning career and living at home in Saltash, that Jack Knapman invited me to ride on the footplate.

Laira shed on 12 September 1959, and somewhat portly Driver Harry Terrell is oiling the cups on the slide bars of 6007 **KING WILLIAM III**. I first knew Harry when a young cleaner boy; Harry was working in the Car Link at that time and he too always invited me up on to the footplate. He was noted for having a very good singing voice, especially between Saltash and Plymouth, and as an 'all-year round' swimmer in the waters off Plymouth Hoe. Terry Nicholls.

Day, the Chargehand Cleaner, who then made the approach to the Head Foreman, Harold Luscombe on my behalf. *Mister* Luscombe – as he was then to all of us – called me in. He was well aware of course that the first railmotor left Saltash at 6.15am but I would be allowed to start the early morning shift at 6.30am and work on half an hour extra to the other lads. Even this meant that I would be late each morning as the motor did not arrive at North Road station till 6.30am and I still had to get to Laira. I cycled down to Saltash station and would put the bike in the luggage compartment of the carriage (or car, as it was known) and stay with it for the ride over the Tamar to North Road. Arriving on one particular morning, I had a shout from the fireman on the engine – was I a cleaner at Laira? Half wondering what I'd done I nodded that it was so. To my bewildered joy I was promptly invited up onto the footplate with him; after all, his driver, Bill Hill, was in the driving vestibule of the leading coach. The fireman's name was Jack Knapman, and in effect he gave me my first ride on the footplate of a steam engine! As I gained a little more experience he permitted me to place some coal on the fire and even showed me how to use the vacuum brake and adjust the reversing lever. Such was the way we began to learn our trade. There is more coincidence in this story, for soon after *Laira Fireman* was published I received a telephone call from a lady in Plymouth who in fact was Jack's daughter, and having purchased the book wanted to know if I knew her dad. I also had the pleasure of meeting with her and

enjoyably exchanging recollections of her father.

Many things sprang from the publication of *Laira Fireman*. I was taken to one side for instance by a former 'man of the footplate' and admonished that in his opinion I had made the footplate seem like 'an Elizabethan drawing room' – all spotless, not a speck of dust to be seen and entirely given an afternoon tea feeling! I am sure that this was not so, and it was certainly remotely not my intention to portray that image. As far as the 'tea' bit went, well yes, we did like our tea, and as often as not the tea can would be replenished whenever an opportunity permitted. Elizabethan drawing room indeed! A strange analogy since none of us had ever been near one, the closest we ever got was Bette Davis in *The Private Lives of Elizabeth and Essex* and some years later *The Virgin Queen* which at least allows me to mention in print for the first and only time in my life and the publications of Irwell Press the wonderful Joan Collins. Far from brocade upholstered seats or 'chintzy' curtains, we had at best hard flip-up wood to sit on and a tarpaulin to stretch between the cab and tender for some protection when for at least half the year it was raining and/or freezing, especially when running tender-first.

To attempt to portray every day on the footplate would be impossible, obviously. Each day was different from the next and yet the same in many ways – as day is to night but with all the vicissitudes inherent therein. The weather was either too hot or too cold, too wet or too dry. The conditions were never 'just right'. Despite this, to answer my

critic I will attempt to describe a 'typical' early turn. In my first book *Laira Fireman*, in Chapter 3, I detailed my promotion from a Cleaner Boy to a fully fledged Fireman. After a spell at Slough engine shed, in the London area, I returned back to my home shed at Laira. Having severed Mother's apron strings, I continued to live in lodging accommodation, in this instance at 19 Percy Terrace, Lipson Vale, Plymouth, the home of Mr (Pop) and Mrs (Ma) Beedle; crucially, it was within walking distance of Laira shed. It was a requirement in those days that members of train crews should, unless special dispensation was given, live within a mile radius of the shed. The Beedles charged me £5 weekly and I was only too glumly aware of how large a chunk this was from my pay packet.

To be a young fireman needing to wake up and leave a warm bed in the early hours of either a wet or cold frosty morning was to hate the alarm clock which roused you from a deep sleep. To ignore it was fatal, but in my case I had an extension to my alarm clock called 'Pop Beedle', my landlady's husband!

Whenever I was on an early turn Pop would always enquire as to what time I would be setting the alarm. I didn't realise for a while but in the early days of lodging with the Beedles, Pop set his alarm for 15 minutes after mine, and would listen for me moving about to ensure that I was not late for my shift. The routine was always the same. My alarm would go off, and like most youngsters I'd turn over – another five minutes wouldn't hurt. Five went to ten and ten to fifteen and then

The Penzance Fireman on 6817 GWENDDWR GRANGE is playing safe collecting the Single Line Token (the 'staff') for the Royal Albert Bridge by lining up his forearm through the 'catching' loop, in the summer of 1952. Some of us liked to show-off if a passenger was watching by grabbing the outer edge of the ring between the thumb and first finger. The signalman in the bridge signal box, watching from his window, is Saltash lad Martin Dennis. Brian A. Butt.

A two-car set waiting on an unusually deserted Saltash station on 10 August 1962. It was unusual for the locomotive to be at the Plymouth end of a two-car Auto train. I wonder if for some reason they were working without the auto gear connected. It could be that the fireman is 'standing in' and is inexperienced in Auto working.

Pop would make his presence felt; a call, a knock which could escalate to 'threats' involving his specially sharpened penknife. I had seen him cut leather to repair his boots with that knife and it went through a layer of leather as though it were paper!

So, out of bed, and after a bite of breakfast, a bleary eyed walk along the path to Lipson Green and the shed. Head tucked down into the collar of my coat to keep the tips of my ears from the freezing cold air and with my warm breath freezing on the lapels. The fingers on my right hand carrying the tin dinner box threatening to fall off as they became colder and colder, and knowing that to change hands would mean that both would then be the same. Booking on there would be an engine to prepare so, yawning my head off as I go to the stores to get the keys for the tool boxes of my locomotive, and even they are frozen. Find the engine in the 'old shed' housing the turntable and silently gave thanks that we were indoors, at least we could have a bit of comfort 'prepping' the engine. The first look would be to see if the engine had any steam at all in the boiler to assist with the preparation.

To have no steam was to breath in the sulphurous fumes which would invade the footplate until sufficient had been raised to work the forced draught (the blower). I'd go into the tender to trim the coal and get some forward for the engine to go off shed; standing amongst the smoke chutes as likely as not I'd be plastered

with years of soot, dislodged every time I banged my head! On any morning in the 'wee small hours', everything you touched on the footplate was metal and cold, including the tools which had to be used. That was apart from the bits that were too hot and burned you. An unlit footplate was always dirtier and dustier, and littered with ash and coal lumps which had spilled forward from the tender, just asking for a turned foot and twisted ankle.

To unlock the tool boxes, with tips of the fingers still numb from carrying the dinner box was a chore. But it revealed the 'flare lamp', a wonderful 'Aladdin's lamp' the company provided, in its concern for our welfare, as a means of light to see as we went about our task. This primitive light had a thick wick stuck in a spout attached to a reservoir filled with paraffin, which when lit, gave off a flame of anywhere between three and six inches in height. Its flickering light was poor and it stank but to us it was the norm. As you light the flare lamp and survey the mess that it is your task to clean up, it is then that you start to wish that you had stayed in bed, whatever the consequences!

If I had arrived a little early there would be time to level the fire part way over the grate and add some lumps of coal, before getting the cans of engine oil, a flare lamp and the 'feeder' (oilcan) down on to the step ready for my mate, to save him climbing on to a dirty footplate. This done, my task was to climb around the

side of the locomotive to check the sand boxes and the smokebox, all cold metal to touch, sweep off any loose smokebox char (in most cases this was brushed through the inspection plate beneath the fire hole) and return to the footplate. The debris would afterwards be shovelled up by a 'shed man'; a labourer. My mate will have arrived and after a greeting to set the mood for the day, would go about his task of inspection and oiling. Removing frozen corks from the oil wells with near frozen fingers is almost an impossibility, and often they would break off – the corks, not the fingers, though sometimes you'd indeed fear for them! A few choice words from the depths beneath the locomotive would indicate that all was not well, and I could imagine him fiddling with a set of implements called 'prickers' and with numb fingers trying to winkle the broken piece out. At last I am starting to get warm as I tend to the fire. With the fire irons (still so cold to the touch that they might almost take your flesh with them) I can gradually build up the fire with lumps of coal, selected with the eye almost of a dry stone wall builder. Soon it would be time to relish the growing warmth coming off the firebox.

As soon as I considered we had steam enough I'd try out the injectors and put some water into the boiler. On one occasion my cold and still slow thinking mind (you only do this once, I can assure you) forgot the driver, oiling away underneath. As I opened the water valves on the tender the steam taps engulfed him in steam and water as they 'blew out' before picking up and working properly. I had originally written that 'to say that he was displeased is putting it mildly.' On reflection this won't do; 'emerging from the pit below like an underworld spirit bent on vengeance' is nearer the mark.

Such disasters aside, all too soon it is time to leave the increasing comfort of the cab to scramble on the tender to bring forward coal from the back, to replenish that used in making up the fire. The driver gets up on the cab for a warm up and fills the sight feed cylinder lubricator. He is in the way now, as I am cleaning up the footplate. Not so straightforward as you'd think. Firstly clear all of the debris underfoot; lumps of coal to the tender, the rest out over the side despite the objections of the shed yardman. Then get the 'pep-pipe' (a water hose) going, and wash down everywhere to clear the dust and dirt. This done, and the fire by now made up, it is time to dry the cab sides with cotton waste, only a bit dirty from previous use. The same stuff, lightly soaked with oil, will serve for wiping down the 'front'; that is, the hot backplate of the firebox which protrudes into the footplate. The idea is this light film of oil will 'fix' any dust flying around on the journey. All is now complete, except for taking on water; it is back now to the cold and wet, clambering over the coal in the tender to put a dripping leather chute ('the bag') into the filling hole of the tender. If it is frozen stiff it has to beaten into submission with a coal pick. Avoid at

all costs a soaking (nothing could be more miserable) as it flails under the water pressure; take it out, running still with the 'afterflow' and throw it over the side taking care to miss your driver.

We're more or less ready to leave the shed now and both of us are alive and alert, recovered from the shock of the cold pre-dawn. We have successfully 'prepped' and kept dry even if a bit raw and cold; after all it could have been raining or snowing! My last task before going off the shed, and perhaps the most important, is to call at the cabin and make a can of tea. A quick hands and face wash with hot water from the boiler in either the bucket or the well of the shovel, and life again starts to feel worth living. Thought can be given to the task ahead. An examination might reveal the odd cut or bruise but it would not be felt at the time; the cure, numbness from the cold came free, courtesy the company!

So life on the footplate was not really as glamorous as you might think, and the point has of course been made many times before. Yet when the rough is weighed against the smooth I think that, in hindsight whether rose-tinted or not, good old smooth wins out. Moreover a young man could shrug off the inconvenience and hardship of early shifts in winter – it meant you were free for a night out – maybe nip over to Saltash to meet up with Joyce.

So, the locomotive 'prepped', tea made, and ready for the off. All is well, or is it? If you are on a tank engine and it is raining 'stair rods' it does not really matter

where you have to go to collect your train. The cab is enclosed and you are sheltered. It's a very different circumstance though, on the open footplate of a tender engine. An engine might leave the shed at Laira in one of two directions. To the east, to Tavistock Junction to work a goods train, presented two rather different options. The first, a job to Newton Abbot and beyond was the more benign, for you left shed the 'right' way; that is, chimney first and comfy in the cab during the sedate run by the banks of the River Plym to the marshalling yard. The second option was a different story. To work a train from that same yard but to the west meant leaving the shed tender first, with no protection at all from the elements bar cowering in your mackintosh. It didn't save you though, you still got wet. And this is before starting out on the train working itself. You stood as close to the fire box as you could, inviting rheumatism, chilblains and other now largely forgotten afflictions your mother warned you against. It was but part of the joy of footplate life.

A passenger working to the west, for a job into Cornwall, was different and the light engine run to Plymouth North Road was chimney first. This was infinitely preferable, for even on a fine clear day without rain, dust would blow back unpleasantly off the coal. On this particular morning we were booked on a train for the east, an up working out of North Road, so it was tender first from the shed to the station. It can seem a long run from Laira to North Road, and an

Walking Time. The route east to the marshalling yards at Tavistock Junction. The tree line at the end of the Plym Estuary in the far distance is adjacent to the western extremity of the sidings. The lines adjacent to the bank of the estuary extend to the Junction and this was where we walked. The road to be used was on the left and can be seen immediately above the finial cap of the signal which is showing as 'off'. R.C. Riley, www.transporttreasury.co.uk

The route to North Road and Millbay entailed walking through the tunnel at Mutley; there it is immediately behind the brake van of the local transfer goods Although pannier tank 3675 has cleared it by a fair distance the smoke can still be seen coming from the tunnel mouth. R. Parkes/C. Horsham.

interminable one when it is raining. So footplate life was governed, at least in its niceties, by the weather, in ways that are often not obvious. Yet there it is, part of the job, the part that the writers of railway tales, and those well-meaning persons advising you to take a job with the Great Western Railway on the footplate, forgot to tell you about!

As the fireman you have to get down between the tender and first carriage to couple up and fate, or the designer of the carriage has decreed, you are standing just beneath the end of the drainage channel taking the rain from the carriage roof, and guess what? Yes, it is directed to fall right on the exposed section of your back between the top of your trousers and the bottom of your jacket which has rode up as you bend forward to pick the coupling!

Trousers hitched, all is forgotten though as we get the 'right away' and settle down to the pleasure of working on what to us was the finest piece of engineering in the world – a Great Western locomotive. Except this time; getting into the gradient of the bank at the bottom of Hemerdon, she does not steam. Out from the rack comes a fire iron to give the fire a bit of a stir-up. 'Fire iron' however, hardly begins to cover it; this, after all, is an inch thick rod of iron maybe *twelve feet* long. This monster was for a King with its 11ft 6ins firebox; the smallest, 6ft for a pannier tank, were not to be sniffed at, either!

They had a ring, perhaps a foot in diameter, at the 'operator end' and is normally stowed horizontally on the tender, the ring sitting over a securing pillar. It is difficult enough to manoeuvre cold. When it is withdrawn from the firebox and ready to be placed back in the rack on the tender, with the right hand in the ring at the end it requires the left hand to grip perhaps three or four feet below the ring to get leverage to swing it backwards and upwards. Somewhat awkwardly, this is the part that has been in the almost white-hot firebox! Gloves were years off on the railway of the 1940s and a wad of cotton waste in that left hand was deemed sufficient protection. It will come as no surprise that the pad sometimes wasn't up to it.

By now you might be wishing for a job for Cornwall instead. Easier down there, excepting perhaps the Royal Albert Bridge where you have to collect the 'staff' on the run. Miss it and you have to stop and trudge back under the gaze of the bemused passengers who are wondering why the train has made an unscheduled stop. In truth you'd be unlucky to miss the staff but it did happen. Alert to the potential humiliation your left hand clutches the ring of the tablet holder in a grip of iron but your mate is trying to make up a bit of time perhaps and runs a bit faster than normal; you haven't noticed this and your left hand, clutching the tablet holder, flies backwards with the

momentum, to hit the side of the tender with the knuckles. And so it goes on.

No such problems for your driver of course who is comfortably settled against the side of the cab, enjoying the day. The stuff of boyhood tales and dreams – to be an engine driver; yet to be an engine driver, *you first of all have to be a fireman.* How did it ever happen?

****

The principal, abiding duty for the fireman was to raise and maintain a copious amount of steam, and keep a safe level of water in the boiler; sufficient for his driver to undertake his side of the job. That is, to work a train from A to B, and in accordance with the timetable and safe working practice. Nothing to it, or was there? Well sometimes, yes, there was, or nearly so, but generally it was not quite so, and for varying reasons.

Firstly, the platform that the fireman worked upon would not stay still, and when a shovel of coal was swung towards the firebox door, it had moved a little to one side or the other from where it had been for the previous shovelful. The shovel then struck the firehole door on one side and the coal spilled on to the footplate which you had worked so hard to keep clear. To help matters this would generally bring a chuckle or derogatory remark from your driver, depending on mood/his disposition towards you. Alright for him, on his seat (well, piece of wood) where the constant variations in the movement of the cab merely meant subtle minor adjustments of the buttocks rather than a bone-jarring clash with the steel rim of the firebox door.

Then of course, the steaming qualities of locomotives differed. Some would steam with a candle in the firebox, it seemed, while on others you could work your heart out to little effect. Conditions could change abruptly; the fire might be burning bright and clear at the start of a job, with the coal close at hand in the tender. This would be especially true of course if it was the engine you'd prepared yourself. Later on though, or on another roster, you could be relieving a train which had left some god-forsaken place who knows how long ago. The fire would be dull and the firebars heavy with clinker; the coal would be dust and dross, far back in the tender.

The steeper the gradient of course, the more steam was used. The more steam used, the more the fireman had to work to provide it. The more he had to provide, the more coal was shovelled into the firebox, and so it went on until his physical limit was reached. In the West Country we had the perfect set of circumstances for the demonstration of all this, the Cornish and South Devon Banks, not forgetting of course both sides of Whiteball on the Devon/Somerset border.

I do not like being too technical, for as I stated in my previous book we did not work to weight per shovel, or shovels per minute. But there were people who did these calculations. I have seen figures of 50-65lb per minute on a normal run, such as Paddington to Taunton. This would increase to about 70lb on the climb to Whiteball, a formidable rate especially if the coal was out of arms reach back in

the tender. Great Western teaching was to use the firehole flap to prevent cold air entering the firebox. Each shovelful would be accompanied by a reach with the left hand to lower the flap, replacing the hand on the shovel for the swing. As the shovel went back towards the tender the left hand would again raise the flap. This was repeated over and over and over again, and most importantly each shovel of coal was directed to a specific part of the firebox and not thrown in, any old way! Each bout of shovelling would be followed by a brush up of the footplate and a damp down of the exposed faces of coal in the tender. I confess that I never took the trouble to weigh a shovelful of coal, but again I have seen it recorded as something like an average of 28lb. I do not know how that works out mathematically over a journey in lb/mile; or tons/hour, but at times I knew it to be, assuredly, a lot!

The fireman moreover was expected, where possible, to assist with the safety of the train; a glance back over the side to see that all was well, looking for certain signals and so on. All in all it could get busy at times… The only respite came on the falling gradients, where although the regulator was not shut completely, there was a chance of a sit-down (unless you had to go into the tender and dig some coal forward). So, who in their right mind would sign up for such a life? Believe it or not, many of us did, and were inexpressibly proud to have done so!

****

A feature of work in the Pilot Link at Laira was relieving crews working on the shunting engines (known as pilots) in the various yards in the Plymouth area. In certain cases one shift would effect a

changeover by taking a 'fresh' engine off shed, the other engine being due in for attention (washout, coaling) which was quite straightforward. For most changeovers the accepted method to reach your locomotive and to effect relief, was by foot after booking on duty at the shed. Pay was calculated from the booking on time, and the period getting to your engine was thus 'paid time'. This was known as 'walking time' and was a specific period (measured in minutes) for every job. It depended on distance of course, but calculated according to the distance from the shed to the respective yard by road or path, not by any rail route. 'Trespassing' on the company's line was forbidden for reasons of safety. The problem was that in all cases it was shorter to walk along the trackside, and therefore a blind eye was turned and crews used the shorter route. This could of course be hazardous, especially in darkness or poor weather. It demanded careful negotiation of all manner of obstacles; rails, points and rodding, signal wires and countless discarded objects such as sleepers and chairs and the like. Walking west to North Road and Millbay meant the passage of Mutley tunnel, often smoke-filled and always wet with water dripping from the roof.

I am not sure how the walking times were arrived at but included within the total was the time taken to 'book on' at the Time Clerks window and to read the relevant notices for the day. To reach the three pilots and the banking engine to the east of Laira at Tavistock Junction for instance, three-quarters of an hour was stipulated. It meant a walk of over a mile and a half by road, but only a mile or so by the track alongside the Plym Estuary, so it was small wonder we opted for the 'short cut'.

The east end of North Road station, 5 July 1955. The many pitfalls of negotiating point rodding and signal wires are self evident. At night or in fog matters were far worse. R.C. Riley, www.transporttreasury.co.uk

Belmont Sidings and the new diesel railcar refuelling and examination depot. R.C. Riley, www.transporttreasury.co.uk

To reach the pilot at Laira yard, adjacent to the engine shed, warranted a walking time of fifteen minutes. To the west, the walk to the North Road station pilot was an hour for a distance of over a mile alongside the track and it was at least half that again by road. It was possible to use a bus if the weather was bad, but payment had to be made from your own pocket, so was accordingly uncommon. The two pilots at Millbay for passenger and goods sidings were allocated an hour and a quarter, while the Millbay Docks pilot merited an hour and a half. Similarly of course, the crews being relieved were afforded the same time allowances for returning to Laira shed to book off duty. This invariably meant that in certain cases crews were required to walk both ways having effected relief at the beginning of the shift and in turn being relieved and then having to return on foot to Laira before booking off duty.

These 'walking times' would not be contemplated today, though they were accepted then as part of the job; it was not worthwhile to establish remote signing on points, with the expense of clerks and so on and this was a sensible way of running the job. Today I don't doubt that railway would hire a taxi or, more likely, abolish the pilot job!

****

Whenever a photographer had been issued with an footplate pass to ride on the locomotive an Inspector would also

be present. This always gave the impression of an overcrowded footplate, but it was not quite like that. Perhaps the best known, and most highly respected by footplatemen during my period was the late Kenneth Leech. He was an enthusiast, the likes of which we shall probably never know again. He developed a love of all things steam during his service as Chief Mechanical Engineer of the Westinghouse Brake and Signal Company; he was also keen to take a turn with the shovel, and was known for his skill on the regulator. Many of his endeavours are documented, (assisted by his great friends Bryan Holden and Dick Potts, a former Tyseley Engineman). It is not my intention to add to them except for one particular journey made by Kenneth on the 26th July 1961 from Plymouth to Paddington. Kenneth has told his story of the journey in his books, *Portrait of Kings* and *A Century in Steam*, but I have always felt that the fireman's account of the trip needs also to be told.

The locomotive was King 4-6-0 6012 KING EDWARD VI of Old Oak Common shed which had worked the Cornish Riviera Limited down from London the previous day. The Laira crew of Driver Edgar Stephens and Fireman W.L. (Bill) Rundle (brother to yours truly) booked on duty to work the first part of the 'Limited', as she was known, to London, to be informed that Kenneth Leech would be travelling on the footplate, overseen by Bill Andress, the Chief Inspector, Swindon.

A fireman would always be acutely conscious of the fact that an inspector was on the footplate, but would be aware that he in turn recognised the important dictum; that the person 'in charge' was in fact the driver. Should he wish to address a fault in the work of the fireman it would be done through the driver. This seldom happened, and normally the conversation with the fireman would be limited to a greeting and a perfunctory inquiry as to his well being. The locomotive had been partly prepared; in the parlance it had been 'done outside', by the morning shift on 'prep' work. It meant that all the tools had been checked and all were present and correct; the lamps had been trimmed and the sand boxes filled and checked to ensure that the sanders were working. The smokebox had been cleaned and the door screwed up tight, and the front splasher brushed clean of smokebox ash. Occasionally the 'prep' fireman would have put a few decent lumps of coal on the fire and got a good few more on to the front of the tender.

A fireman had an allotted time of one hour for the full preparation; the work included making up the fire, trimming the tender, having a good tidy up and ensuring cleanliness of the footplate. Before leaving the shed the tender would be filled with water and if required, topped up with coal. The fireman, Bill, had noticed that the 'prep' fireman had spilled sand on the splasher framing around the sandbox and had not brushed it off. It was Bill's intention to remedy this. It was not so small a matter as you might think; he did not want dry sand blowing back towards the cab on the run, it could get in your eyes. But in all of the hustle and bustle of photographer and inspector, he forgot to sweep it away. Half a century on he is still mortified that Kenneth's subsequent pictures show this sand most clearly – a blemish on a proud career preserved for ever! Inspector Bill Andress and Kenneth Leech finally climbed up on to the footplate, and KING EDWARD VI and its four men rumbled off shed to North Road station, and there coupled up to the train.

'Right away' duly came and the locomotive was working normally, responding to Bill's efforts and steaming freely; all was in good order. Running down to Aller Junction and Newton Abbot, my brother Bill caught a comment from the inspector to his driver: 'Get us to Paddington on time, Edgar, I don't want to miss my train back home'. This was official approval to 'go at it' and those (like the inspector) who knew Edgar to be of the 'enthusiastic' school of enginemanship, knew that this was all the encouragement he needed. Newton Abbot, Exeter, up the climb to Whiteball and all was in first class order. Inspector Andress had taken up the approved position behind the driver, content with

an occasional aside; he was perfectly happy with the footplate work.

Kenneth Leech had been taking an occasional photograph from the edge of the footplate, but other than a word to Bill Andress had not made much conversation. Through Whiteball tunnel and Edgar, picking up speed as the front of the engine dropped on the downward gradient, shut the regulator with a flourish, opened it again to the 'drift' position to keep lubricating oil flowing into the cylinders, and sat down for the run to Taunton. Edgar checked the speed through Wellington station and, as the falling gradient lessened at Norton Fitzwarren, started to bring the cut-off back to something around 12-15% and opened up the regulator for the run into Taunton. With the bells ringing in the cab to tell of the distant signals off and a clear run for the 'through road' at Taunton station, the lever was brought back to 12½% and the regulator was put on the second port, the driver's hand on the chain whistle all the way. Now there were no doors between cab and tender on a GW locomotive and all of a sudden fireman Bill noticed that Kenneth Leech was hanging out over the side, still wearing his trilby hat and raincoat, at a speed approaching 80 mph. He was filming the run to the station, oblivious

to all else. The inspector remarked, almost resignedly: 'We're going to lose him one of these days – he'll go out over the side!' To the fireman it was remarkable for the inspector to confide in him in that manner, but he had to agree with the estimation of the photographer's prospects. Kenneth seemed quite unperturbed and calmly completed his filming.

Working the tender in the best of Western tradition, shovelling from the middle and then to the sides where the best of the 'nubbly' coal was always to be found, Bill had been able to keep a bright fire and a full head of steam quite comfortably. They took water at Creech troughs and were by now firing steadily for the rising gradient to Somerton tunnel, through Castle Cary and on to the pull through Bruton. There were gradients of 1 in 70/80 to the summit at Brewham and the load was ten coaches; through Westbury and with the long drag up to Savernake, Bill had hit a batch of small coal and as reported in Kenneth's book *Portrait of Kings*, 'it was also full of dust forming a clinging, paste-like substance on the shovel. In the firebox it either went straight up the chimney, or else ran back on to the firebars as clinker.'

For Bill everything had, literally as well as metaphorically, turned to dust. To his mind it was more than just bad coal,

The most-distant pilot job to be relieved and thus the furthest walk was the docks below Millbay where the little 1361 class 0-6-0STs reigned supreme. By now the sight of the locomotive, wood seat or not, was a most welcome one - anywhere to get off your feet! They went back to Laira for servicing, like 1363 by the coal stage around 1960. A. Scarsbrook, Initial Photographics.

Photographer and Laira Driver Les Kingwell stand in front of 'Dockie' 1363 at Sutton Pool on 3 June 1961. Terry was Clerk to the Area Foreman at that time. Terry Nicholls.

steam valve. It was much easier than working a lever and allowing the sand to trickle down under gravity, as on the Great Western. I always felt though, that if the aim was to overcome the problems of a wet rail, then surely the introduction of steam would aggravate the problem, and undo any benefit from the sand. Yet it obviously worked.

The very fine sand used by the Great Western came from West Wales and was delivered to the engine sheds in fifteen ton wagons. Each shed had a 'sand house' with a large hopper and fire grate inside. The sand would be shovelled into the hopper and dried over the fire so that it trickled freely into a bin ready for collection by firemen as required. On GW engines this fine sand was carried in sand boxes slung beneath the running plate, immediately above the leading edge of the front driving wheels and behind the trailing driving wheels. From the box a pipe fed the sand to the rail. The sand was delivered using a lever on the floor of the footplate, on the driver's side on tender engines and the fireman's side on tank engines. The weakness of the Great Western system was that the sand had to be absolutely dry to flow once the lever opened the valve, and one of the fireman's tasks when 'prepping' a locomotive was to ensure that the sand was running. Often as not, and especially in wet weather, the delivery pipes gathered up moisture whilst travelling, and the sand would clog in the pipe. The usual way to clear it was a sharp couple of taps with a spanner or coal pick on the pipes; the damp sand would dislodge, clearing the way for the dry stuff in the box to flow. This was straightforward enough standing on the shed, though there were legends of firemen clambering out to do this out on the road! We were masters in the art of 'leg-pulling', and stories told in the enginemen's cabin could sometimes be a little exaggerated...

Many of the stories would feature an incident, conveniently impossible to verify by date, record or witness, on the down journey from Newton Abbot, on one of the South Devon banks of Dainton or Rattery. They traditionally involved a heavily laden coal train; the circumstances were invariably malign! The story would centre around a poorly steaming locomotive, probably a 28XX class 2-8-0 with a home shed in South Wales; Severn Tunnel Junction or some similarly barbarous place, which had been on the road for at least a week or more. The tender would have been raked over and

though no other possible reason was apparent. The clock had dropped back off the mark, the water was falling in the glass. Time to get a fire iron out of the rack and give the fire a stir-up, and at the same time look for a fault, a hole in the fire perhaps. To his experienced eye, all seemed in order and the fire was properly hot at the front. Struggling to the top at Savernake with steam pressure falling off and water getting low, they could not help but lose time.

From here it was either level or falling track all of the way to Paddington, and with Bill using all of his firing knowledge and Edgar aware of the problems his fireman was encountering, KING EDWARD VI was nursed along until the steaming problem was overcome, simply by continued effort and attention. It seemed simply to pass, as such problems did, inexplicably. Steaming duly returned to near normal. With the steam and water back as it should be, and after taking on a last refill of water from the troughs beyond Newbury, Bill was able to relax and think about the last lap of the journey to Paddington. Kenneth Leech recounts

in one of his books how Edgar Stephens had driven 6012 for a fair amount of the way with only 12½%. Bill had been made aware of this at Maidenhead, Inspector Andress remarking that he 'didn't know these b——ds would go so fast wound back to 12½%!' The lost time was steadily notched up, and more was made up by Paddington so that the train arrived in London a full twelve minutes early. Only when the fire was worked down did the cause of the poor steaming reveal itself. The first two rows of the brick arch had dropped down in the front end of the firebox. This was the hottest part of the fire where temperatures could reach as much as 2,500 degrees Fahrenheit. As Bill Andress remarked whilst getting down from the footplate, 'that accounts for that then boy, don't it?'

Earlier on I mentioned the errant sand on the running plate of 6012, fireman Bill Rundle's public disgrace. On the Great Western we did not have the 'steam sanders' used by the other companies. In this method the sand used to prevent the locomotive from slipping on a wet rail was forced there under pressure using a over by successive firemen and all of the decent coal used until only dross remained. To compound the problems it would be raining of course, and the rails wet. As the luckless but inevitably bold and daring crew came up to the last couple of hundred yards or so to Dainton Tunnel (or if on the other bank, around Tigley) she'd 'start to slip'. Working the sand levers would not have had the desired effect, so nobly and without any thought for personal safety, the fireman would have grabbed his coal pick, swung out over the side and dropped down on to the track. The wheels would be flashing round and the connecting rods almost a blur. Paramount, of course, was the imperative need to ensure that his train arrived at Tavistock Junction, no matter what. He'd hammer away at the sand pipes in a selfless mission to clear them and get some sand on to the rails to give the wheels a grip.

The practical difficulties were insurmountable of course, not least keeping your footing at the side of a ballasted track sloping sharply away. A stumble was inevitable; stumbling the wrong way, into the wheels, would have been fatal. Yet for the tale-teller this derring-do would have the desired effect, with disaster narrowly averted. The wheels, against all hope, would 'pick up' once more, the fireman could leap back on the footplate to the plaudits of his admiring driver, and probably hear a whistle in acknowledgement from the crew of the banker engine at the rear of train, who had been in no doubt that the entire weight of the train was on their front end. To double to the drama, the story-teller might decide that the first exploit was not successful, and would

have the fireman returning to the footplate to exchange the coal pick for the coal shovel…

This truly was above and beyond the call of duty. Abandoning all reason, the fireman's task was then to *climb back down again* and use the shovel to gather up suitably sized lumps of ballast and then to throw that on the rail in front of the leading driving wheels. Well, what a good idea. Listening intently, the only flaw that I could see was the somewhat tricky task of selecting the right material to be used. After all, while all of this was happening on the trackside the locomotive was still slipping on the rail with forward motion fading fast. The driver up on the footplate would be using all of *his* expertise, of course while relying on his fireman to use his somewhat unconventional athletic skills, and do something to help.

To return to *The Terror of the Tracks*: The fireman on the ground throwing shovelfuls of debris on to the rail belatedly wonders if this was a good idea. The debris of course is bound to contain stones of varying sizes. Those not of a nature to be squashed under the locomotive wheels would be ricocheted out to the side and fly past the fireman's head and ears like bullets. And it would not be just one, more like a salvo. Anyone would have to be half mad to even think about it, much less do it and wholly mad to expect anyone to believe it. Yet there was, as always, some truth to all this and I myself had got a 'stranded' engine going – it was not all that uncommon. Yes, there was a down coal train and yes it was a 28XX from Severn Tunnel Junction and of course the coal was rubbish and yes we slipped after a shower of rain fell on to the track above Stoneycombe, on the

approach to the tunnel. But this is where the truth veers off somewhat from that cabin tale. No driver would take such a chance with the safety of his fireman and my driver, Claude Bolt, did not let me to get down from the footplate until we had slipped to a standstill. Yes I tried to get the sanders working by rapping at them with the coal pick, all to no avail. It was then that Claude suggested we 'sand' the rails with some earthy material from the side of the track and we did this for a considerable distance, avoiding any 'boulders'. After a while Claude decided that we had done enough, and returning to the footplate, again sounded the requisite 'double crow' signal to the banking engine, and off we went again. Well, our old 28XX started to slip immediately but, inch by inch we got a gradual forward movement. At last though, she got hold of the debris we had placed on the rail and 'Praise Be' started to work with her wheels. With just an occasional slip, we eventually reached the top at Dainton. Claude looked at me and with a smile: 'Well done, we made it', was all he said.

Oh, I almost forgot. Yes the debris on the track did ricochet all over the place. It would have been a daft place to have been down there though, and I was much better off, and safer, on the footplate watching and listening!

****

During the Second World War it was considered prudent that, in case of an emergency, the train crews of both the Great Western and Southern Railways should be familiar with each other's route between Plymouth and Exeter. To this end

Terry Nicholls standing on the footplate of 1364 on 17 September 1958. 1363. Terry Nicholls

Exchange workings – this is Friary, the Southern station, around 1955. A WR 2-6-0 stands in front of SR M7 0-4-4T 30036, the station pilot, waiting to couple on to the coaches of the train that will work over the Southern rails to Exeter Central.

in 1942 there appeared 'exchange diagrams' whereby certain of the drivers from Plymouth Laira and Friary, and Exeter GW and Exmouth Junction were travelling on the footplate of each other's locomotives 'learning the road'. For many years the sea wall at Dawlish, so much a feature of the Great Western line, had been the cause of disruption in the winter, when heavy rainfall, high winds and extreme tides could flood the track there. The Southern line to the north, threading the boundaries of Dartmoor, could fall prey to snow. Either route of course, at any time, could be blocked by derailments or other blockages. Before the days of wholesale branch line closures in the West the GWR/WR had its own alternative route, of sorts, from Exeter to Newton Abbot via the branch from Exeter St Thomas through Trusham and Chudleigh to Heathfield, and then down the Moretonhampstead line to Newton Abbot. Although not suitable for express locomotives, the carriages of the trains could be worked by the smaller classes, and at least some sort of a service could be run. The most obviously useful way of diverting trains remained the two main lines and the formal 'exchange diagrams' ensured that crews got the regular experience that meant they could work any trains when circumstances demanded it. The workings involved one crew from each of the four sheds. Exeter Western Region shed had the 11.47 am Exeter Central to Friary, returning with the 4.40 pm Friary-Exeter Central 'stopper' and Laira the 2.25 pm Friary-Exeter Central, similarly a 'stopper', returning with the 6.35 pm Exeter Central to Friary 'semi

fast'. For the Southern Region Exmouth Junction worked the 11.25am Exeter St David's to Plymouth North Road, returning with the 4.27 pm Plymouth to Exeter St David's. Friary shed, the SR's Plymouth establishment, had the 2.15 pm Plymouth-Exeter St David's, returning with the 5.30 pm Exeter St David's to Plymouth North Road.

One time in 1955 I was booked on an afternoon 'spare turn' and was surprised upon checking the 'sheets' to find that I 'had a job', and was not to be just stuck in the shed labouring. My turn was in the No.2 Passenger Link, paired with Driver Albert Stansbury, the 2.25 pm Friary to Exeter Central and return, over the Southern rails and thus an entirely new experience.

Booking on was, I recall 1.0 pm, to 'get an engine ready' but, eager to impress, I arrived half an hour before time. The larger GW types were too wide for the Southern loading limits so the engine was to be one of Laira's 53XX mixed traffic 2-6-0s, 5376. My previous experience on these engines had mostly been with goods trains, and in the main I'd found them to be free-steaming and good to fire. When working hard on the banks they had a distinctive roll from side to side, and when shovelling coal it was easy to time the swing of the shovel to coincide with that movement.

I was well into my preparation when Albert, my driver, arrived and after exchanging the usual introductions employed by newly paired mates, 5376 was made ready for the road. The obligatory can of tea was secured as the final task before we made our way to the 'speedway', the 'off shed' road at the south-west end of Laira adjacent to the roads serving the straight four road 'New Shed'. I had naturally informed Albert that this was to be a 'first time' for me, not having worked over the Southern before, and got an assurance that I was not to worry. He would be ready with whatever help and advice I'd need as we went along.

Running tender first into Friary we were directed on to the three or four carriages that would form our train and I went to place the headlamp, for a stopping train code, on the front bracket. Albert quietly corrected me – this was the Southern after all and 'they did things different to us!' The SR code for a stopping passenger was more like ours for a goods train, 'Code 'H'. This was one lamp on the top by the chimney and a second beneath it on the centre lamp bracket of the buffer beam.

Waiting for 'right away' Albert let me know that his regular mate would be away all week so, all being well, this turn would be mine until Friday. He also revealed a little of the nature of the Southern road. It was a case of boiler management to great degree he said. He made the point that the first stretch to St Budeaux would seem familiar as it mingled with our own route. From there it fell down to the level stretch alongside the River Tamar to Taw viaduct across the mouth of the River Tavy. From there it was a rising gradient all of the way to Meldon near to Okehampton. Once at Okehampton, he said, it was down hill all of the way to Exeter St David's. I had heard of the severe climb from St David's up to Central.

We left Friary station dead on time and worked our way to North Road, passing Laira shed on the way. I was warned to be careful that I did not 'over fire' along the next stretch; at the same time a full boiler of water and head of steam would be an advantage when we left the Tamar, together with a 'bright' fire. Somehow I got it wrong, and though I'd managed the first two successfully by the Taw Bridge, the fire in the firebox certainly wasn't 'bright'. In my eagerness to have a good body of fire for the climb to Meldon, I had overdone it. By Bere Ferrers and Bere Alston the steam pressure was only just holding up, but it would fade fast from thereon as the gradient came to something like 1 in 73 or so. So it was the standard recourse to fire iron and a good stir-up for the fire. Sacrificing water for steam I concentrated on the fire, determined to get it right.

A stop of reasonable length at Tavistock helped to redress the problem, and Albert suggested that I should try to

A Southern T9 4-4-0 with a train for Exeter Central runs past the engine shed at Friary. The photographer is standing on the single platform of Lucas Terrace Halt – it was a case of 'alight here for the shed'. It served the single line branch round to Plymstock and Turnchapel. The recreation ground – 'the rec' – lies in front of the house of St Judes. A. Lathey, www.transporttrreasury.co.uk

control the water level in the boiler and let it come down to something like a half a glass by Meldon. This would prevent the engine from blowing off excessive steam for the 1 in 77 run down to Cowley Bridge junction and the Western main line to Exeter. By now I had got the footplate, or at least my part of it, sorted out and life became a little easier and there was time to admire the scenery. Although (naturally) not comparable with Cornwall, the Devon countryside is quite spectacular on this stretch of the Southern.

From Tavistock we ran 'entwined' with the Western rails from Mary Tavy to Lydford, where there was a shared station and signal box. We were climbing steadily now and 5376 started to 'roll' as the pressure made itself felt in the two cylinders. With a stop at Bridestowe followed by Meldon Junction, the hard work was done for a bit, and there was a chance to tidy up, and have a sit down. Over the magnificent Meldon Viaduct, with the junction for Halwill, from where it seemed possible to travel to the ends of the earth, or at least to Devon and Cornwall, and on to Okehampton. It was a falling gradient now to Sampford Courtenay, North Tawton and Bow and all I needed to do in addition to keeping a look out for signals and so on was to put the injector on to stop the engine from 'blowing-off', and place an occasional shovel of coal in the box to keep the back end full. Through Yeoford, Crediton, Newton St Cyres and Cowley Junction and all too soon we reached Exeter St David's. Here we had to pick up a banking engine, despite the light load, for the fearsome 1 in 33 incline up to Central and the final stop. That section was just one hard up-hill 'blast', and very memorable. At central we uncoupled and proceeded forward to the shed at Exmouth Junction to turn the locomotive ready for the return train at 6.35 pm. I have to say that I enjoyed the experience immensely, and

especially so after I had sorted myself out and started to fire the engine as I had been taught.

Albert put things into perspective, declaring (a bit tongue in cheek) that that was just the 'learning bit', and that I would do it properly going back to Friary! And do you know? I believe that I did just that. Albert must have been satisfied, for, after eventually reaching Friary, and leaving our coaching stock, he quietly said to me on the run to Laira, 'well, young Phil, I think you've earned the right to be here for the rest of the week. I'll see the foreman when we get back to shed'.

Whilst writing this I suddenly realised that no matter how long since Nationalisation, we still looked upon them as the Southern *Railway* and not Southern Region.

Right. **West Country Pacific 34001 EXETER approaching Lucas Terrace in the course of turning on the Southern's triangle Mount Gould/Cattewater Junction on 23 June 1949 after working over the Western route from Exeter St David's through Newton Abbot to Plymouth North Road. The Pacifics were too big for Friary's turntable and had to use either the Cattewater or Lipson triangles. After completing the turn the locomotive will travel back to North Road for the return working. Beyond, to the right of the engine, is Embankment Road, the River Plym and the Sutton harbour line. The houses of Mount Gould occupy the slopes to the left and, in front, is the east end of the recreation ground seen in the background to the T9 at Friary. S.C. Nash.**

The 4.10pm Plymouth Friary to Exeter Central running past the Lipson curve by the Great Western's Laira shed, headed by 2-6-0 6385. This was in fact the return working for the Western crew from Exeter St David's shed. R.E. Vincent, www.transporttrreasury.co.uk

One of Laira's finest, 6029 KING EDWARD VIII, bursts forth from Parsons Rock tunnel by Dawlish with an express from London, bound for Plymouth, about 1955. T.G. Hepburn, Rail Archive Stephenson.

The western land spans of the Royal Albert Bridge at Saltash on the 28 September 1957, 4-6-0 6970 WHADDON HALL heading The Royal Duchy as it leaves Cornwall behind, for the long journey to Paddington where she is due to arrive at 7.15pm. L. Elsey.

Chapter 2
Owls and Fish

Railways were very keen on publicity and public relations, long before it was called 'PR'. The naming of locomotives, trains and services, with variously heroic/romantic/noble antecedents was very much part of this and the Great Western was to the fore. Trains were loosely 'categorised', and the term 'passenger' could mean express, stopping or branch. On 'our' railway the Royal Mail through train, the Travelling Post Office (TPO) was called the 'postal'. Ocean Liner Specials had been known as a 'mail trains' from the earliest days. A passenger train with a Royal Mail van attached became 'North Mail', etc depending on its destination or origin. A freight was a 'goods' whether a through working or a pick-up stopping everywhere; coal and minerals were just that. A 'perishable' could encompass parcels, fish, milk, flowers and fruit and almost anything else. The only exceptions to this practice of not naming trains quite for what they were seem to have been Royal Trains.

At some time deep in the past railwaymen began to give certain express passenger trains nicknames, some of which 'stuck', and came to be used officially – like the Cornishman, the 10.50 am for Penzance, the Flying Dutchman and the Zulu, both for Plymouth. Others never attained official status, such as the Flying Welshman, the North Star and the Owl (inevitably a night sleeper, 12 midnight off Paddington for Penzance). The Cornish Riviera Limited (started in 1904; left London at 10.30am) was the most prominent that I recall, but others included the Torbay Express for Torquay and Kingswear, the Royal Duchy and the Mayflower, both for Penzance. There were quite a few more over the years.

'Express' goods trains, worked most notably perhaps by the big 47XX 2-8-0s which were always to me the 'Kings' of goods working, also attracted nicknames which may even have adopted officially, or at least semi-officially. Those serving the West of England included the 10.55pm Bristol to Laira ('the Drake'); the 9.32pm Old Oak Common-Penzance ('the Cornishman'); the 4.58pm Marazion-Bristol ('Tre Pol and Pen Flyer'); the 10.10pm Paddington-Laira ('the Tamar'); 7.20 Penzance-Tavistock Junction ('the Pasty' which became the 6.25am Tavistock Junction to Paddington but whether it remained the Pasty – who knows?!); 2.50pm Penzance-Paddington ('the Searchlight'); 10.30pm Reading-Laira ('the Biscuit'); the 3.50 Swindon-Tavistock Junction known as 'the Rasher' and the 9.55pm Westbury to Penzance known as 'the Western Flash.'

None of these ancient institutions lasted long enough to attract modern names – the Burger perhaps or the Flying Nugget.

The Cornish Riviera Express, although grand sounding, was ever abbreviated on the railway to the 'Limited', a reference back to the days when the loading was limited to a set number of through carriages plus a couple of slip carriages. The train took some four hours for the non-stop run to Plymouth and, before the practice was abandoned, 'slipped' coaches for Weymouth (at Westbury), for Ilfracombe (at Taunton) and for Exeter. This last portion served the intermediate stations to Newton Abbot. In the 1950s the train ran in anything up to four parts, with through portions for Newquay and Falmouth and for St Ives. Engine changes for those two Cornwall portions were carried out at Newton Abbot, with locomotives from Cornish sheds taking over, leaving the engines which had worked down from Plymouth to attach as pilots for the main train and to assist her over the banks to Plymouth. At one time the Kings would change over at Keyham West End, leaving the engine and crew to travel all of the way to Laira tender first.

As a young Cornish lad I was in the Church Hall at St Mewan for some sort of function, when I could not help but overhear a conversation between two of the ladies of our Parish. Although brought up not to eavesdrop, I could not help but hear what was said.

'Ere' said the first lady, 'Av' you 'ad your 'air done, then?'

'Aise' replied the second lady, 'Jim and me be goin' off to Lunnon'.

Castle class 5049 EARL OF PLYMOUTH at Swindon shed on 6 September 1959, after a heavy intermediate at the Works and ready to go to its then home Newton Abbot. It should have been one of ours of course but instead whiled away its time at places like Worcester and Canton, only coming briefly 'home' for a few months over 1956-57. Up until then the good Earl was not a regular visitor to Plymouth at all but when the engine did appear it was of course accorded every respect. Well, not really; instead was always called 'The Undertaker', after a well known firm of undertakers in the city. R.C. Riley, www.transporttreasury.co.uk

Perhaps the most famous of all trains for the Cornish Road, coupled with one of the longest name plates of a Great Western locomotive. Laira Castle 5069 ISAMBARD KINGDOM BRUNEL is on the up Cornish Riviera Express at St Erth on 14 August 1958. A.E. Bennett, www.transporttreasury.co.uk

The up Travelling Post Office (TPO) passing Marazion in GW days with 5059 EARL ST. ALDWYN at the front. The date is not recorded, for though the doctor could recall all the dates with ease, he never wrote them down! This would have been a return working for the Laira crew and locomotive who worked the down 'Riviera' from Plymouth. Dr Ian C. Allen, www.transporttreasury.co.uk

'Darnee' said the first, 'Ow be ee goin' up there then, by coach?'

'Bless my soul no' said the second lady, Jim's gone and booked us on the Riverra, no less.'

'The Riverra?, be 'ee sure? Must have cost a pretty penny.'

'Well aise, s'pose it did, but Jim, he 'ad a little windfall, don't 'ee knaw, and 't'was his idea to go to Lunnon, and what 'ee think, us be travelling up on the Riverra'.

'The Riverra' repeated the first lady, disbelieving. 'Naw 'ee be 'aving me on!', and stomped away.

I now went home and told my mum the story, and asked her what the 'Riverra' might be.

'Bless my soul Philip, that be the special train on the Great Western Railway, the Cornish Riviera Limited, and only posh people can afford to ride on that train'. As I grew older I came to realise that to the people of Cornwall held the 'Limited' in high esteem. To them she was always *The Riverra*.

****

Signal boxes usually carried their name on the front wall, on a prominent board. Crews could always check where they were! While putting together these notes I came across two interesting ones. 'Dr Day's Bridge Junction Signal Box of unusual length and the amusing 'Box Signal Box' near Bath.

The 'home shed' of any Great Western locomotive in pre-nationalisation days could easily be recognised by the letters painted on the running plate immediately behind the front buffer plate. The three or so letters were an abbreviation of the shed name and became quite distinctive.

The only exceptions were Old Oak Common where the letters PDN (an abbreviation of Paddington, where the original shed had been) were used instead and Shrewsbury – SALOP. The rest were fairly straightforward; SLO – Slough (my first shed as a fireman); RDG – Reading; DID – Didcot; OXF – Oxford; LA – Laira; SBZ – St. Blazey; TR – Truro; PZ – Penzance. And so on.

A railwayman's job title could also cause confusion. I recall at Slough that we worked turns called 'zonal duties'. Upon booking on Dai, my driver, would contact the Area Control Office by telephone, and then wait for instructions. Within the Office there was more than one Controller, each covering his own section which were known as 'Districts'; I'll standardise on 'Area'. We were there at the convenience of 'Control' to relieve crews on overtime or long hours, working specials or whatever and thus avoiding them working longer than determined by their shift. Much of it was just wait, and wait, and wait, in the shed until released to go home. If we did move, we could be sent anywhere, subject only to the driver's knowledge of the road. I do not think that we fully appreciated the importance of Control; to us it just seemed at times to 'interfere' in the smooth running of the railway, inconveniencing us wherever it could. It was Control who decided if a goods train might hinder a passenger train's clear road; on the other hand if it thought prudent, Control ordered it out of the way to let the passenger through. It is little known that District Controllers had responsibilities beyond the actual movement of trains; they also had to be aware of the wagons held in local goods

yards and arrange the local pick-up goods to call to move them to the marshalling yards for forwarding on. The need for footplate crews to exchange engines at times could prove a headache, for trains had to arrive in the right place and at the correct time to effect the changeover.

A special working would on occasion be required in order to clear an excess of say, empty wagons and this often did not suit all 'sides'. A shed foremen would have to find a locomotive and crew and while Control would be aware of men on 'spare turns', and locomotives in principle available on shed', the shed foreman would inevitably have his own ideas for how they should be employed and heated discussions would sometimes ensue. It is a pity that some of these conversations were never recorded for posterity. Or perhaps not.

In the No.2 Goods Link one time, we were working the 4.25 pick-up goods from Tavistock Junction into Cornwall. We'd shunt all stations west of Saltash with a goods yard and were booked to 'swap' footplates with a Cornish crew working east with the 5.50 am 'H' class goods from Penzance. The changeover was supposed to be at Doublebois but if we were running late the Cornish men came to Menheniot, and did they moan. On one occasion we had to go down over Largin to Bodmin Road (and did *we* moan). Control took the blame, though no one there probably had anything to do with the fact that shunting took longer than was scheduled! They came in for a lot of 'stick', yet credit to them in hindsight, they generally got it right!

Express 'through' passenger trains dominated the workings of the shed at Laira while it was clay trains that fulfilled

Penzance station on 6 September 1956, the up Travelling Post Office (TPO or, more usually, 'the 'Postal' to those who worked the train) loading with mail prior to departure at 6.40pm. This is still some time ahead, by the look of it. It is not often realised that in the case of TPOs the whole train, not just the locomotive, had to be turned before the return run, requiring sometimes a considerable run out to the nearest triangle. Eric Sawford, www.transporttreasury.co.uk

the same role at St Blazey shed. Penzance and Newton Abbot had their own jealously guarded top passenger work while Truro and Penzance could justifiably lay claim to the best of the work so far as the fruit of the sea and the land was concerned. After passengers, high-value 'perishable' foodstuffs, the price highly dependent on the season and its weather, came next in the hierarchy, as judged by Control.

With the development of the railway in Cornwall outlets for Cornish produce acquired an undreamed-of importance. Now for the first time the migrating shoals could be caught in abundance and sent straight to market in London and the Midlands; the mild winters meant early fruit, flowers and veg could be forwarded to the centres of population, at a premium price.

The mackerel and pilchards caught in the seas off the coast of Cornwall attracted a huge demand especially in London. *The West Briton* newspaper reported in 1879 that on a particular Friday, no less than four trains of vans left Cornwall for the fish market at Billingsgate. Fish swimming in the Cornish waters on Friday, it was claimed, could be bought from the stalls at Billingsgate on Saturday morning. This was a revolutionary development and though it all might now go by road, the railways established our present day consumer economy. The trade continued into the early 1960s, when all such traffics disappeared from the railway.

Such was the demand that at times additional vans would also be attached to through passenger trains. The harbour at Newlyn expanded greatly, with trawlers from as far afield as Lowestoft coming to take part in this fishing 'bonanza'. This in itself brought additional revenue to the railway, 'stimulating trade' in a classic virtuous circle; the large trawlers of the time were powered by steam, and the Great Western duly brought coal from South Wales to feed their boilers. Expansion saw additional Cornish and Devonshire harbours, notably amongst them St Ives, Padstow, Newquay, Mevagissey and Brixham – all served by the railway – join in the new prosperity.

The Isles of Scilly sent over boxed flowers for transport to Covent Garden and the Cornish flower growers, from Lands End to the Tamar Valley, took advantage of their own mild climate to follow suit a week or so later. The traffic flows followed the joyful advance of spring; every day gained over competitors further east meant a better price. In the mid-1880s Cornish farmers turned large expanses of arable land over to the growing of broccoli, and the endless trains hauling specially cleaned cattle wagons loaded to the roofs with crates of this exclusive vegetable (it didn't figure as part of the 'greens' on many working class plates) are legendary. The yards on the Helston branch and at Marazion in the season were completely taken over for this trade. The movement of broccoli 'specials' was given a reasonable degree of priority; the cattle wagons were vacuum braked which meant that these trains could be run on a schedule equal to a parcels train. I have told in *Laira Fireman* the story of the banking of these trains up the Hemerdon Bank, east of Plympton, and how at night the procession was virtually continuous for the two banking engines. The return to Tavistock Junction after assisting one broccoli special to the top would mean passing the second banker blasting its way up; once back down another 'special' would be waiting.

The growers on the Scillies were not content just with flowers and were renowned for their new potatoes, the 'Jerseys' which in the first few weeks before competitors' produce arrived were too expensive for most mums to even think of for their shopping baskets. This traffic came to equal, and most probably surpass, the broccoli trade. Cornwall had its own new potato industry; greengrocers all over the country still called them 'Jerseys' but no one complained, the housewife was just glad they'd suddenly become cheaper! Goods yards in the west got back the clean cattle wagons as the broccoli trade faded and now stuffed them with sacks of Cornish new potatoes. Again the Helston branch was busy with this industry, the yard at Penryn sending away vast quantities.

The weather could upset all of the forward planning. An early frost could cause a delay in the readiness of the

Right. A long way from her home shed of Westbury, 5985 MOSTYN HALL is working the afternoon Kensington milk train, the 12.20 ex-Penzance on 10 July 1955. The location is just west of Liskeard. R.C. Riley, www.transporttreasury.co.uk

Below. On the afternoon of 3 October 1959 the fireman of 4950 PATSHULL HALL leans out to hang the staff on to the 'bull-horn' arm attached to the Royal Albert Bridge signal box. The 'third rail' between the rails of the adjacent track is the GWR ATC (Automatic Train Control) ramp which activated the contact shoe under the locomotive, to give an indication of the signal in the cab. The train is the 12.20pm Penzance to Kensington 'milk'. Terry Nicholls.

crops for harvesting and if careful attention was not given snow could interfere with the movement of the cattle wagons to the various yards. Some of these yards were not very big, for they saw modest use for most of the years; stabling too many wagons could result in a yard being unable to cope with normal everyday traffic.

In the engine sheds, as in the Traffic Department on the Great Western (the arrangements on the other companies were surely similar) there was an in-built capacity to cope with unlooked-for demands. In most Links, excepting perhaps the top passenger ones, the schedules included 'spare turns' to cover every hour of the day and night. The main reason for this was of course to cover for holidays and sickness as well as any emergency that should arise. In the summer season it was these crews that helped to cater for the additional seasonal Trains.

Being 'spare' as we called it could be a lot more interesting and rewarding than it might sound. The railway seemed to attract all manner of custom and whole farms have been known to be moved from one county to another, lock stock and barrel, from the rails of one company to another. Livestock, farm implements, animal fodder and fertiliser all required differing handling and wagons. Tree trunks hewn from the woods, pit props for the coal mines cut into suitable lengths, were transported literally in their millions. The range of industrial equipment was endless and included such things as large power generators to ships propellers.

An unwelcome traffic was the offal, carcasses, hides and bones from abattoirs which went by rail, and this was certainly a regular feature in Cornwall and the West in general, where many country stations had their own slaughterhouses. Ruth Batchelor, who was a booking clerk at Doublebois station, west of Liskeard in Cornwall, tells how the sidings at Doublebois were not only used extensively for the conveyance of pit props from the nearby Duchy of Cornwall Forestry, but was also a favourite marshalling point for the vile smelling offal wagons. Ruth recalls that the smell at times, and especially in hot weather was almost unbearable; truly sickening. Inexplicably, even when the wagons had departed the smell still lingered. Ruth now lives at St Blazey in Cornwall having been married to Carey, a former St Blazey driver.

I am reminded that these wagons were hated by train crews, and in particular the goods guards. Working regulations decreed that wagons of this nature should be coupled at the rear of the train in front of the brake van, with its thoroughly disconsolate guard inside! One can only imagine the discomfort; it was bad enough when stationary, but with the forward movement of the train, the nauseating stink would invade its way through the far from hermetically sealed wooden van doors, and there would be no getting away from it.

The whole business was thoroughly disgusting and whenever one of these noxious wagons was stationary for any length of time and then moved on, the spot where it had been standing would have the outline of the wagon shown on the ground by a host of maggots which had been shaken out from between its boards. Shunters and enginemen talk of the sidings at Cattedown in Plymouth, the destination for the wagons. The ground would be absolutely covered by these unwelcome guests after the offal had been loaded on to coasters for shipment to the glue factory. It was no consolation to a guard that the lot of a seaman on these ships was far worse! Fish wagons too, stank, the empties leaving a rotten miasma in their wake, but they never approached the awfulness of the offal wagons.

The railway even shifted the travelling circus, and I recall as a young lad seeing Billy Smart's Circus coming to St Austell, unloading in the dock behind the station. To a child the length of the train and its sheer scale was astounding, and the wagons which bore the animal cages seemed outlandish. The lions, tigers and so on were carried in their cages on long 'Crocodile' well wagons, which had a low-sung central section. The elephants were in immense covered vans, as befitted their size. These wagons in turn were known as 'Pythons' and as with the Crocodiles the name was painted clearly on the side. These I took to be specialist circus wagons though of course they weren't – all wagons had 'animal' telegraph code names, quite by chance. They'd seemed appropriate to me at the time, though it was disappointing that the elephants were in the pythons' wagon!

To watch the unloading of the cages and seeing them lifted on to carts and lorries for hauling to Rocky Park on the western outskirts of the town, was unbelievably exciting. My great fear was that a cage might fall off or a door spring open with the ferocious animals breaking free to eat everyone. The elephants were led away from their vast covered trailer. They seemed used to all the upset and slowly ambled on to the bay platform and then the long walk to join with the rest of the circus, entirely unconcerned. If there had been trees or bushes along the way, I swear they would have swiped the odd trunkload to eat.

In addition to the wagons with the animals there were others which carried the great marquee, the smaller tents and seating, stacked with a precision so remarkable everything was clearly designed to break down into components that exactly fitted the wagons. Flat wagons carried the circus vehicles and an assortment of caravans, all in the garish colours and slogans of the circus.

The West Country was a great milk producing area, and Cornish dairy produce has a reputation second to none. Almost from the beginnings of the railway dairy farmers and milk factories made use of it for the rich new markets to the east of the Tamar, first in churns, then in tanker wagons. The Great Western at one time sent over 200,000 gallons daily to London, from Wales as well as the West Country. This trade was highly prized by the Great Western and special instructions were in place to ensure that the milk was not unduly impeded on its run to the capital. Each day two trains left Penzance, normally made up with an unspecified number of milk tanks behind the locomotive and a guards/parcels van. Where additional loadings of milk churns were indicated, an additional 'Siphon G' would be added in front of the guards/parcels van. Butter, cream and cheeses went in the guards/parcels van. There were additional pick-ups on the way, including the milk factories at St Erth and Lostwithiel, Saltash and Totnes.

****

The West Country holiday trade has been well documented, and the GW was not slow in its methods of attracting holiday makers to the resorts of South Devon and Cornwall. Special trains, even those that took your motor car as well as yourself, added to an already comprehensive passenger timetable. This inevitably led to 'queuing up' west of Exeter on a summer Saturday. All this placed an enormous pressure upon the operation of the line, and all involved in it. Always there was the fear that some minor derailment at some crucial point would throw everything into complete chaos. The most difficult burden I always felt (I would, after all) fell upon the men and machines that actually worked those additional trains.

What has saddened me most over the years since 1948 is the way the railways have lost almost entirely the transport of heavy goods. I accept that the improved road systems and motorways have won, completely, but still feel that the place for the bulkiest stuff – steel, coal and minerals – should not be on lorries but on rail. But then, I am naturally biased, and make no apology for it. Oh! 'by the way', I hear you ask, 'what did you do when you left the railway?' Believe it or not, I gained qualifications in Highway Engineering, working for the enemy for the rest of my career!

Economy of working. At the west end of the bridge, on 13 August 1962, the two-car Plymouth to Saltash auto train has an empty milk tanker tacked on the front. This will be placed in a siding at the west end of Saltash station, where it will be filled with milk from the creameries beneath the bridge, alongside the River Tamar. It was usual for two tankers each day to be despatched from Saltash for Kensington, but in order to save the through train from stopping they were forwarded to Plymouth through this simple expedient, attaching it to a suitable auto service. Bill Potter.

Exeter St. David's on 20 July 1956, with 0-6-0 2230 shunting milk tankers in preparation for collection by a through Kensington milk train. That last mile or two on the milk float to the doorstep was the least part of milk's long journey R.C. Riley, www.transporttreasury.co.uk

The Isles of Scilly maintained close links with the mainland dating back to 1858 when the first ferry service commenced. This of course gave an opportunity to the Islanders to develop their market gardening, opening up enormously greater outlets for the produce, and also attracting tourists. The records show that the first shipment of just 50 boxes of flowers came in 1880, where now the shipments are measured in tons. This image (a bit shaky, I confess) shows that when the flowers had to be gathered it became a task for every member of the family. The men and boys worked in the fields and did the picking while wives and daughters undertook the sorting and the packaging ready for export. Once ashore, most of the output went by rail to London and the Midlands.

Loading Cornish broccoli in the goods sidings at Marazion 9 April 1960. Broccoli was possibly the 'ultimate' of the Cornish produce, a premium product beyond the purse of many – in the days before our fruit and veg came from all over the world it did not figure in the shopping basket of the ordinary housewife. Large tracts of rich Cornish land was given up for this exotic greenstuff. It was estimated that in 1939 alone 73 special trains left the west of Cornwall in just one week with produce destined for markets east of the county. R. C. Riley, www.transporttreasury.co.uk

5002 LUDLOW CASTLE working one the slowest Parcels trains to run through Cornwall. Leaving Penzance at 4.50pm it called at all but the minor stations to either set down or pick-up, and did not reach Plymouth until 8.40pm. Leaving with just a few vehicles, by the time it finished collecting additional vans it would have a full load for the eventual climb up Largin Bank; indeed it might well need assistance at some places. Its eventual destination was paddington. Dr Ian C. Allen, www.transporttreasury.co.uk

It might be thought unusual to include in a chapter mainly concerned with 'double-home' working, an image of an auto train on a service for the Tavistock branch – no staying away on this job! In fact it is not the train, though the sidings beyond the single carriage is where the 'Cars' for the suburban service were stabled. No, in one of those sidings once lurked the exclusive, select (some said malodorous) lodging accommodation for the crews from Old Oak Common and elsewhere, working a double home shift. It was an old sagging sleeping car with a second carriage for the kitchen, permanently stabled in these sidings and convenient for all the clanging, banging and ear-splitting blowing off in the shed yard all day and night. Not to mention passing trains. It was thus not unknown for London crews to make private arrangements in local houses. View is of 64XX 0-6-0PT 6400, on 1 December 1962. Terry Nicholls.

Chapter 3
Home Front, Lodging

At a recent Retired Members meeting, I managed briefly to stop Ruth Batchelor and Joyce Rundle from talking, and Vi Giles from selling raffle tickets, to ask a question that had long been in my mind, faint-heartedness having hitherto prevented me asking it. Just how did the wives feel about being married to railwaymen – guards, shunters, footplatemen and the rest?

Ruth, sadly now widowed, had been married to Carey, a driver at St Blazey shed but she was a railwayman in her own right, having worked for the Great Western as a booking clerk at Doublebois station. Joyce is my sister in law and something of a heroine in the family for taking brother Bill off of our hands. He needs no introduction; we heard earlier of his trip to London with 6012 KING EDWARD VI and he featured prominently in *Laira Fireman*. I greatly value his advice and comments, but can't let him know it! Vi, also widowed, was married to Bob Giles, a much respected driver at Laira, and to whom my brother fired at one time. I tell her story at the end of this section.

As it turned out I didn't need to fear the answer to my question but all three ladies agreed that the biggest difficulty was coming to terms with 'unsocial' hours. It meant a 'normal' way of life was impossible in as much as planning ahead became difficult. A railwayman's shift patterns were not conducive to a regular social life and proved particularly irksome when the husband was on 'spare turns', when a duty could be moved two hours either way. Moreover when a man was working nights, there was the ever-present need for some quiet around the house while the husband slept. It meant tip-toeing around the rooms and the impossible job of keeping children's noise down.

Washing work clothes was a chore. It was a fact of the job that for some reason the smell of oil and smoke was always present no matter how careful a man was with his personal toiletry. It was ingrained, and there were no showers or baths at the shed when a man came off duty. He went home as dirty as when he stepped off the footplate. It wasn't exactly

Three 'steam wives'. Left Ruth Bachelor, married Carey (St Blazey); middle Violet (Vi) Giles, married Bob (Laira) and Joyce Rundle, married Bill (Laira). Sadly, Both Ruth and Vi were widowed during the preparation of this book, and regretfully Vi has now died and is being very much missed.

Fireman Grainger and Driver Carey Batchelor, smoking his pipe, standing against the nameplate of 4-6-0 1002 COUNTY OF BERKS from Penzance shed, on 23 September 1960. R.C. Riley, www.transporttreasury.co.uk

House of ill-omen. No.44 Well House Road, London NW10. Better known as 'Hilda's'. This was one of the double-home lodging houses at Old Oak Common before the hostel was built. Martin Budd.

unpleasant, the ladies recalled diplomatically, but one was ever conscious of it. It must be remembered that in those days and indeed into the 1960s working people did not change clothes or take a bath on a daily basis. It simply wasn't done, for making hot water to bathe and wash clothes was a tedious and expensive operation, especially in the crowded conditions of the times. Council houses with the hitherto unimagined luxury of a bath *room* only began to be built after the War.

The smell of coal and oil invaded a man's working clothes, but the inconvenience differed according to where you lived. Joyce had a laundry close by and the worst soiled items such as overalls were despatched there, with the rest done in the weekly wash, strictly separate from the 'whites' of course. Ruth, living in a cottage at St Blazey, far from the urban sophistication of Plymouth, made do with the rural 'wash day' which I remember so well as a boy. The weekly wash meant getting up at (or before, in winter) the crack of dawn to fill up 'the copper' with water, sometimes fetched from the adjacent stream or well. Light the fire, and then it might be back to bed for a couple of hours while the water boiled. In to the copper went washing powder, 'Sylvan Flakes' or some such long forgotten brand. Clothes were sorted as to the degree of dirtiness – lightly soiled was washed first, and so on with the railway overalls for a certainty being

boiled and washed last in the order of things. 'Agitation' came courtesy of a cut-off broom handle, and was very hard work. Many a time boiling in the copper did not produce the hoped for results, and Ruth had to resort to getting the hand scrubbing brush, and a bar of hard soap; the cure for all ills in those days. The overalls were laid on a flat surface and the dirt scrubbed out of them. It did nothing for the life for the material but it always had the desired effect. Even mud splattered young lads had the 'bar of hard soap' treatment as I can readily confirm.

Rinsing was done in separate baths filled ready with clean water; into one would go the 'whites' where the water had been treated with a 'blue bag' to make the clothes 'whiter than white' as the TV would tell you some years later. After rinsing, the clothes were then introduced to the 'mangle' – a forbidding, medieval apparatus comprised of two large wooden rollers set in a cast iron frame and turned by a handle set in a large wheel. The clothes went through the rollers which squeezed every last drop of moisture from them, and the were hung out to dry on the clothes line set up in the garden. Two posts with a length of cord slung between them attached to pulleys which lifted the clothes high into the air to dry. Perhaps the footplate life was easier!

Vi's weekly wash went straight into the copper for a boiling, and then a good scrubbing on the washboard. Bob's

'whites – underclothes and things' had to be changed every day. They would be black and certainly tested the manufacturers' claims for certain brands of washing powder.

I asked if they were concerned if their husband did not arrive home within a reasonable time. I knew that at Laira the Old Road Inn among others could prove a distraction, especially on pay-day. But there were operational delays; mishaps and worse and my thoughts were that accidents did happen. Some were fatal, like the runaway at Burngullow and I wondered if such thoughts were in Ruth's mind especially. Both agreed that such worries always surfaced, especially if a man was long over due, for there was no way of communicating any news. Ruth too was haunted by that runaway if Carey was on the Burngullow turn and was late home.

Next I wondered, a bit hesitantly, what happened when the 'other half' went to bed in the early evening for an early shift, perhaps 2 or 3am? Were they concerned not to disturb the sleeper when they retired for the night? Joyce recalled that when Bill went to sleep he went 'deado', and little would disturb him, but like many shift workers he had a knack of coming completely awake the moment the alarm went off. She would go to bed at her normal time for going to bed. Ruth, in her cottage, did not see the point of staying down on her own, so she would get Carey's sandwiches or whatever ready for him to take to work in the morning and go to bed too.

Lastly, I was interested if the husbands used the services of the shed call-boy, a junior cleaner whose job was to make the rounds of all men on early turn, knocking on doors, ringing bells, or throwing gravel at bedroom windows. Did he wake our ladies' men, and them too in the process? Like wives the world over they were able to turn over and go back to sleep once more.

Violet Giles ('Bob always called me by my full name – but you can call me Vi') was from a railway family. Father Sidney Jones had been a goods guard at Laira so by the time of her marriage to Bob she was well used to the man of the house working 'odd' hours. Her brother was also on the railway, as engine cleaner at Laira, and that was how she met Bob. They started courting in 1945; in the aftermath of the war it was difficult for them to get any accommodation, which meant the engagement lasted seven years until their marriage in 1952.

Violet Giles was emphatic that her Bob 'lived for the railway', and was proud to be a Great Western man, something my brother was able to confirm. He was a very caring, quiet and thoughtful man; Violet recalls: 'he was good as gold, I could not wish for a better marriage, no one could ever replace him'. Bob died in May 2003, having worked all but two weeks of 44 years on the railway. He was an engine driver for 26 of those years. Bob was known for always planning ahead. On Monday he would not be thinking of the present weeks shift, but what he would be working the following week.

On the footplate while fireman Bill, my brother, would be thinking of stopping at the next station, Bob would suddenly talk about two or three stops ahead. Coming down from Newton Abbot with Dainton the first bank to be tackled, the discussion would be about Rattery bank many miles ahead. Vi sadly has died in 2011, a great loss to us all.

Railway work stayed in the family and Bob's father too had been an engine driver; usual practice was that two members of the same family should not work on the same footplate, but somehow Bob fired to his father for two years when in the Top Link at Laira. He also lodged at 'Hilda's' (see later) and was a great enthusiast for the Railway Social Club at Laira. Violet and Bob spent many an hour down there 'seeing to things' as she put it; checking stock, generally tidying up, sorting out the club notice board and so on. Bob was also much involved in the original organisation of the 'Christmas Santa Special Charity Train' which ran from Plymouth to Calstock every year. My great friend Don Lee was the 'Father Christmas' on the train. Vi said that the specials only stopped when British Rail withdrew the 'gift' of the train – if it had to be paid for at commercial rates there'd be no money left for charity. Bah, humbug!

'Mateship' was vital to footplate work; Brother Bill for instance, observed that when he fired to Tommy Marsh he spent more hours of the day with him, than he did with his wife Joyce! It was the same for all three ladies, Joyce observing that if Bill had said 'waking hours' this would certainly be true for the night shift, where the off-duty hours in the day was spent asleep.

All of this of course was the same for the wives of all train crews. I am also certain that my former colleagues would echo my sentiments, that we could not have done our job without their support.

It was good leaving the shed after a hard shift and walk home knowing that they would be waiting for our arrival. Shouldn't let them know that though, there will be no living with them!

'Double home working', which meant 'lodging' overnight or during the day before your next duty home, was detested by some crews while others could hardly get enough of it. You either loved it or you hated it. The thought of being away from home for a night did not rest easy in some minds, especially perhaps the fireman who was in all probability a young married man with a young family. This did not mean that those who held no objection to this class of work, liked it because it got them away from 'the missus'! I am sure that was not the case, mostly anyway; they just enjoyed that challenge of the one journey for one day.

In fact, at Laira as in all top links, the double home work (in our case to London) was seen as the 'icing on the cake'. This work set you above all others, putting you among the elite and, of course, it paid well. It attracted 'mileage rate'; 140 miles was reckoned as being worth a normal days pay, and every fifteen miles beyond that meant an extra hour of pay. Remember, Paddington was 225 miles from Plymouth, so London's streets really were paved with gold! Working to London from Laira could almost double a man's pay. Penzance and back meant ten hours pay, as did Taunton. Yet the London money was well and truly earned! The fireman shovelled some five or six tons of coal, observed signals and attended to the husbandry of the footplate. The driver, familiar with every section of the track, every change in gradient, had to read endless signals; everything had to be acted upon accordingly. The opening and shutting of the regulator, adjusted up and down, recalled the proverbial 'fiddlers elbow'. A 'reversing lever' which controlled the length of the stroke of the

piston according to the demands of the road and loading would be lovingly (maybe) adjusted a myriad of times, and all of this while keeping an eye on the other side of the footplate to see how things were over there.

It was not just the part that the paying public saw; there was the preparation time getting the engine ready at Laira before going into North Road station for the train. Then at Paddington, the 'official' journey done, there was the run back to Old Oak Common. Once there, if necessary, the driver would place a 'repair sheet' in for the fitters for any defects which might have appeared during the run. A minor 'run of the mill' repair would be done while we lodged, with the locomotive ready for the return to Plymouth the following shift.

And that shift, of all, had its own special problems for the fireman; after a near-194 mile slog from Paddington to Newton Abbot, he'd be getting weary, with the coal, dauntingly, 'way back' in the tender. It needed shovelling twice to get it in the firebox. The fire by now is beginning to form clinker on the bars, all the tea has gone, and the South Devon banks await! Doesn't seem to be fair does it? But that was The Job.

No trip with a steam locomotive was ever really the same; a comparative 'doddle' on a fine day with good coal and a free-steamer in tip-top condition could turn nightmarish in poor weather on an ailing locomotive. It is my humble opinion, never admitted in public, that at both Paddington and Plymouth, Old Oak and Laira men alike felt a sense of relief that 'we've got here'.

At Laira shed the 6.25am Tavistock Junction (the Marsh Mills sidings) to Paddington was a 'Fast' freight train of perishable goods which the Laira crews originally worked to Taunton, returning the same day with a similar train. In the 1950s the powers-that-be decided to

Large Prairie 2-6-2T 3186 standing by the hoist at Laira shed. Used mainly for banking trains on Hemerdon, she is the sister engine to 3187 which was 'shunted' through the west wall of the Old Shed.

introduce 'double-home' workings (that is, the crews 'lodged' for twelve or so hours before returning) on selected freight trains. Two of these trains were being considered, the 6.25am from London, and the second the 1.30am Tavistock Junction-Bristol returning the following day with the 9.45pm Bristol-Tavistock Junction.

Although at Laira we had come to accept double home work as a necessary evil (though some preferred it) for express passenger trains to London, it was felt that this was going a step too far. It was especially so in the case of the fireman who in the majority of cases would be a young man, newly married and in all probability starting a family. To take them away from their homes for additional nights did not seem right. An appraisal of the proposed working schedules saw Westbury considered as a double home destination but this was not going to be productive for either BR or the train crews. As long as the engine shed at Taunton was in operation, why alter the existing satisfactory arrangements whereby the train was worked to there and the crew relieved by the Taunton men, with a return working home to Plymouth the same day. Some of the Laira men affected even felt that considering that Plymouth to Paddington was a days work involving some 225 miles excluding to and from the sheds, Tavistock Junction to Westbury and return would work out only a little longer at something like 260 miles. Similarly, the Bristol and return the same day approximated to something like 250 miles.

Numerous meetings ensued between the Staff Representatives and British Railways officials; heels dug in all round but BR was determined upon implementing these workings, to the point, it was felt, of intransigence on the part of BR. Workforce hearts became very much inflamed and threats of 'withdrawal of labour' were duly muttered. So far it had been a local matter and when local officials at Laira contacted the HQ of the union, the Associated Society of Locomotive Engineers and Firemen, much to their surprise and disgust the necessary approval and hoped-for national support was not forthcoming. The General Secretary even visited Laira to personally inform the members there that BR's plans would not be opposed. His message was quite clear; 'if you strike, it will be unofficial and unsupported'. Faced with this the Laira men had no option but to accept the new workings.

I have not been able to obtain clarification on the lodging arrangements at Westbury for the Laira crews but as I received no complaints in that direction I can only assume that they were satisfactory. What was irksome were the arrangements made to work the return journey. Rather than re-route the 8.55pm to Westbury in order to effect the change over of crews, the Laira men were required to walk to Heywood Road Junction and change over with the Old Oak Common men at that point. There were two alternatives. Either walk alongside the track which was full of obstacles or take a short cut across a

couple of fields. Either way not so clever in rain or snow and while waiting the only shelter was a small lineside internal phone box, probably put there for use when the slip coach arrived from the down 'Limited'.

The lodgings on the Bristol turn was called the Old Rectory, but it was not as commodious or genteel as it might sound. It was not to everyone's liking with the driver, fireman and guard all sleeping in the same room. Worse still, the return working arrived at Tavistock Junction at 2.30am. Laira men swapped with a Penzance crew and once back home, after being away from home for the best part of two days, were required to tramp the track alongside the Estuary of the River Plym for the best part of a mile to Laira shed to book off. As we all know, winds off estuaries can be very unpleasant indeed.

****

An Old Oak Common crew worked to Plymouth one day and the fireman was unfortunately taken ill. Laira foreman Fred Manley informed my brother Bill that he was to work the sick man's train to London and then return home 'on the cushions' – that is, as a passenger. The train was an afternoon 'mail' with a Royal Mail van attached, and went via Bristol. Although the foreman's instructions were quite clear, somewhere lines had got crossed, for when the train arrived at Bristol Temple Meads station a Bath Road fireman climbed up and announced that he was Bill's relief. A little disappointed, Bill got down from the footplate and wandered across the platforms to the down side to catch the next passenger train back to Plymouth. One duly arrived and Bill got into the first compartment of the leading coach, where an elderly gentleman was already ensconced. They nodded at each other and as the train started away Bill settled down for forty winks.

The gent caught his eye and inquired if Bill was 'on the footplate'. This of course was so, and it turned out the old chap had been a driver. Earlier, as a fireman at Exeter he had worked double homes to Truro, something unknown in our time. Furthermore on the return journey from Truro they stopped at the top of St Germans bank to have brakes pinned down. I cannot find anyone left at Laira, St Blazey, Truro or Penzance who when working an *up* goods stopped at the top of St Germans bank to pin down brakes. This man claims to have worked over the section of line between Wearde Signal Box and St Germans which was a part of the original Cornwall Railway and before the deviation was constructed through Shillingham Tunnel. The deviation opened in 1905. He had to be a 'fair old age'!

In *Laira Fireman* I wrote of one of the lodging houses close by Old Oak Common shed, known as 'Hilda's'. I am grateful to Martin Budd, son of the late Stanley E. Budd, a former driver at Old Oak, who now resides in the 'Duchy' at Bodmin. Martin, born in 1938, recalls his boyhood in London and his home at No.26 Wells House Road, London NW10.

Now Hilda had No.44 and Martin remembers several of the houses in Wells House Road serving as lodgings for double home men, who came from all points of the GW compass. It was a traditional way for railway widows to earn a little extra 'letting out the spare room'. As Martin relates, one spare room it was. The terraced houses were all the same, with three bedrooms. There was one at the front, the double-size 'best', a single room and a 'box' in which a bed could be shoe-horned. You got in at night by the back door, using a key hung on a piece of string inside the letter box, or under a flower pot or some similar arrangement.

I have been fortunate to meet with a retired driver, Norman Williams, now 90 years of age, who actually can recall staying at Hilda's. I have told Norman's full story in Chapter Nine, but will relate here the connection with Hilda's. They worked up one day on the 3.45 pm from Plymouth via Bristol. After putting the locomotive away on shed, driver and fireman made the long walk to Wells House Road and No.44, ready to fall into bed. But it was not to be. Once the key had been fished out and the door opened, the first job was to light a candle. There was gas lighting but to use it might incur Hilda's wrath. The candle was enough to illuminate a large *slate* notice board which had all the look of the official about it. The first instruction was to take your boots off and leave them by the door. There was no prospect of a welcoming cup of tea.

The instructions were plain and brooked no argument. 'Laira Crew up 3.45' (that was Norman and his mate alright) were allotted 'Room 2' but only 'when vacated' by the crew already asleep in it, *in the beds*. They would be getting up soon for a Paddington departure, for Wales maybe, or they might be Laira men. So it was a wait until a crew left the room before you could get to bed, slipping in between the rumpled and still warm sheets. You just had to hope the previous occupant didn't have a personal hygiene problem. On one occasion it was a Laira crew, and the fireman was Ken Ryder. Not only was the bed still warm when they got in, and the chamber pot already partly full, but the pillow cases were black with the stains of coal dust and Brylcreem, a favourite hair dressing for young men in those days. It gets worse; the footplate crew shared the double bed, and the guard had one of the other rooms. Demarcation was all!

As a young lad, and having fired a locomotive from Plymouth, Norman was always ready for sleep and would have 'kipped' down on the floor if necessary. No one thought to question the arrangements and indeed such 'private' lodgings were often preferable to some of the official 'barracks' that the railways provided. These were built on company property for cheapness; if this meant siting it next to the coaling plant with all the banging and noise going on day and night, then so be it.

Hilda, it turns out, did not actually live in No.44, but would come in during the

The inevitable small prairie, this time 5515 on 8.8am to Falmouth waiting to leave Truro on 29 May 1960.   L.R. Freeman, www.transporttreasury.co.uk

mornings to have a clean and 'tidy up'. On his second firing trip to London, Norman was having his breakfast in the 'front' room downstairs, when another Plymouth driver, Bill Nance, told Norman to help himself to a second cuppa from the pot on the next table. Thinking what a nice gesture that had been, Norman picked up the tea pot and started to pour it; suddenly the door flew open and there stood the unnervingly percipient Hilda. She tore him off a strip and demanded to know what the now-terrified Norman thought he was doing. It seems that the ration was one cup of tea with the breakfast. Bill Nance new this and dropped Norman in it for the laugh.

Perhaps time rounds off the sharp edges and Hilda is now remembered as a kindlier person than perhaps she really was. It was a different time in so many ways, and her way of doing things was simply accepted and no one saw any reason to alter or improve. Nowadays such conditions would not be tolerated for an instant but then was then, and now is now. Happily not all double home lodgings were like that, and Hilda's was

the exception rather than the rule. With the War came lengthier, more disrupted shifts; modern lodging houses with individual rooms and 24 hour canteens were built, with properly looked after and – such a luxury! – properly laundered rooms.

After all these years a couple of further points are worth noting. Neither Norman nor his driver ever paid any money to Hilda for their lodging, so she presumably had some contract with the Great Western at Old Oak Common. The name 'double homes' was a misnomer; the system effectively meant being away from your home for two whole days. The railway gave no thought to, or made any provision for food for those crews on arrival at London, or once they had left Hilda's, to sustain them on the way home.

When I returned to Laira after completing my stint of National Service, I found that my 'seniority' had been maintained in the meantime and that I had been promoted into the No.2 Goods Link with Claude Bolt as my driver. I was a little surprised to find that in my absence there had been some adjustments to the

link workings. Amongst other small changes I found that the Tavistock Junction banking engines which I had worked in the Pilot Link had been transferred into No.2 Goods, so I was to have a second spell on them. Not that I minded for I found that type of work interesting.

As coincidence would have it I was rostered on a banking turn only a couple of weeks after returning to the railway. The engine was 3187, a big 2-6-2T and I could not help but observe that it had suffered an over-enthusiastic 'buffering up' or maybe a minor collision. Thus the running plate was distorted; from the front buffer beam back to the water tanks there was a noticeable upward swing, perhaps a little more pronounced on the drivers side than mine. It did not seem to affect her working as far as I could tell, but I was puzzled as to how it had happened. After all there is a great deal of strengthened steel there, not withstanding the two stays from the firebox saddle to the buffer beam. The version I heard was that it had been caused by an excess of banking work, which didn't seem right to me. 3187's

before being stabled in one of the outside sidings ready to work back to South Wales or somewhere just as distant. Now these simple and cheaply built locomotives, intended for work in liberated Europe and designed to be 'disposable', nevertheless lasted more or less to the end of steam. They were nothing if not strong, and inevitably had a different braking system to that which we enjoyed; moreover the controls were very basic, as their name suggests, and did not have the 'finesse' of the Western locos.

It seems that, as per normal practice, the shed turner was bringing the locomotive from the stage to the turntable. The turntable was old and not really big enough and large tender engines like a WD had to be balanced exactly, or it would be very hard to push. On this occasion 3187 was stabled on the short road opposite the 'in' road, on the far side of the 'table. The Austerity was brought slowly on until it was almost balanced and just needed a little touch on the regulator to get it perfectly positioned. The WD regulator was not a sensitive instrument, as I've said and opened much more than the hapless turner expected. The result was that the locomotive leapt forward off the turntable, on to the stabling road and was halted only by 3187, hitting her with such force that she jolted backward in defiance of the handbrake. The big prairie tank jumped the small stop blocks at the end of the road and struck the shed wall with sufficient force to punch her front end through before coming to a stop. It was a most unfortunate mishap and could have happened to any one of us. My first thoughts were of my own days on shed turning, and thinking *there but for the Grace of God…* There must have been an enquiry of sorts but no one was harmed (there could easily have been injuries or worse) and it would have been quietly resolved. Shed foremen were railway men themselves after all and the non-GW Austerity regulator could be blamed as at least partly the culprit. No doubt a lesson was learnt concerning the handling of these 'foreign' 2-8-0s. After all that was what the Pilot Link was all about, learning your trade.

Cabs were open affairs on the (G)WR which was fine in decent weather; the only protection provided against driving rain, snow and general tempest on the footplate (especially when running in reverse) was a sheet of 'weatherproof' tarpaulin which could be fixed to the back of the cab roof by small hooks and was fastened to brackets on the front of the tender by rope ties. In the No.2 Goods Link at Laira with Claude Bolt my driver, we were stuck one pitch dark, miserable, rainy night in the loop at Aller Junction with a down goods for Tavistock Junction. We had one of the said cab sheet in position which characteristically offered little protection from the elements, and I had been back into the tender to bring some coal forward for the journey westwards and home. While there I unintentionally knocked the sheet, which had a sag where rainwater had collected. This promptly cascaded all over me. At times in those days I had an 'angry young man' side to

my character and this time I certainly lived up to it, with a stream of curses, 'useless' and 'uncomfortable' seeming the lack the necessary rigour.

Now Claude was a very quiet and well-spoken man, and did not take kindly to this. He promptly ordered me to 'pipe down' and to sit on my seat and shut up, which I did, soaking wet and seething. I was then treated to a lecture the like of which I had never experienced. Claude did not raise his voice once, used no undue words, and quietly stopped me from talking when I tried to interrupt. I was getting a telling off, and in no uncertain manner. As I calmed down and listened to him, I realised that he was not admonishing me for my use of foul language, but in effect my use of *the phrases useless and uncomfortable.*

Firstly he informed me that the Great Western footplate was not made for comfort. If I wanted that perhaps I should have joined our neighbours at Friary! He reminded me that this was our workplace, and although Spartan compared to some of the footplates of our 'rivals', it was probably the most functional. He even went so far as to tell me that while I had been firing to him, I had carried out my work satisfactorily, so there could not be much wrong with the footplate. He then came to the matter of the cab sheet. Quietly he informed me that only a few years previously that good honest cab sheet I was cursing could possibly have been responsible for saving the lives of footplatemen and to call it useless was to denigrate its use during the war. It seems that a directive came out from Paddington that footplates should be blacked out to prevent the glare from the firebox attracting the attention of the German aircraft at night. To do this they adapted the cab sheet by extending it and incorporating side flaps. Claude pointed out that you had to work with them in place to appreciate just how much they really interfered with the working of the footplate back then.

To get a fire iron or to place it back in the tender rack was to become entangled. When the night was warm and 'balmy' the crew sweltered within, where no cooling air could reach, and when rainy the sheet dripped with condensation. The driver was unable to look over the side to ascertain where he was, or to stop with certainty at a station platform. But, he emphasised, what was that compared to the centre of an aircraft's cannon sights? By the time he had finished I was a somewhat chastened if still wet young man. It was possible to regard the sheet in a new light after that, but was still glad when we didn't need one!

fellow bankers 3186 and 5148 had suffered no similar distortion, and in general all of the banking work was shared equally between the three. Perhaps 5148 got off most lightly because she was also a regular engine on an early morning pick-up goods into Cornwall.

I found out, by accident/sleuthing, what were probably the real circumstances. To get to Laira shed from my lodgings in Percy Terrace, Lipson Vale, I used to walk the footpath alongside the parkland at the western edge of the shed, which eventually gave access to the path leading to the shed entrance. Walking to work in that first week back I could not help but notice a large area of fresh brickwork in the western wall of what was the 'Old Shed', the roundhouse built back in the days of William Dean, with a turntable in the middle. Not true to any shape and stretching from ground to the roof, it was evident that something untoward had happened. Making enquiries of the Boilermakers, whose cabin was adjacent, I solved the mystery.

It turned out that the shed turners had a WD 'Austerity' class 2-8-0 coming off the coal stage, which had to be turned

And a big one. Large prairie 4167 at Par with train for Newquay (Cornish Riviera Express – the 'Riverra' in the up platform) on 17 August 1958. A.E. Bennett, www.transporttreasuy.co.uk

Devonport station. This was where I commenced my railway career whilst waiting for a vacancy to occur at Laira. The portal of the tunnel can just be seen behind the grassy bank on the right, and it never failed to amaze me that underneath *our* tunnel ran the Southern Railway, also in a tunnel. R. Parkes/C. Horsham.

A look at the Royal Albert Bridge, from the east end of the down platform at Saltash in June 1958. I recall that when working the Cornish road I always experienced a slight apprehension on the approach as to whether I would miss picking up the staff. This feared disaster only came to pass on one occasion. And I'm sticking to my story. The great bridge is 'framed' by the end of Warleigh Villas and the trees growing on land below the first land span of the bridge in Albert Road. The housing at the foot of the picture is of the former Waterside area of Saltash fronting the foreshore. This was a 'warren' of houses and alley-ways in which he 'Watersiders' as they were known resided. The livelihood of men of Waterside were mainly connected with the river – salmon, net fishing or similar. The whole area was demolished and rebuilt under the Waterside Redevelopment Scheme in 1957.

Chapter 4
The Cornish Road

It was not my original intention to include the working over the line from Plymouth to Penzance. As the content for this book developed I found, however, that some detail should be forthcoming to put the work of the Cornish sheds in context. The Cornish Road has been likened to the cutting edge of a saw, but whereas the teeth in a saw are evenly matched the profile between Plymouth and Penzance most surely is not. It is more like an elongated 'roller-coaster'.

In Chapter 5 I give credit to the manner of train handling on the gradients of the branch lines in Cornwall, by crews from St Blazey, Truro and Penzance; no less skill was required on the main line. A Laira crew working west from Plymouth are confronted with a 1 in 31 rising gradient up to Devonport and the tunnel. The crew of a goods train, of course, had already had one rising section, from Laira Junction to Mutley tunnel to liven up the fire, but for the passenger train crew this is their chance to see how the locomotive is going to respond. If all is well the fireman has taken the opportunity to add to his already bright fire and to ensure that an even layer is now covering two-thirds of the front end of the firebox and that the back corners are well and truly full.

Once through the tunnel, which in fact runs over the top of the Southern Railway main line to Exeter, the line falls to Keyham and St Budeaux East signal box.

The regulator is lifted for the short steep climb of 1in 58/59 to the Royal Albert Bridge. There the 'staff', the single line token, will be collected and there is a chance to top up the boiler, have a tidy up, damp down the footplate and raise a fuller head of steam for the road west of Saltash. A quick touch on the whistle as we come out of the western portal lets my wife in our house above know that I am coming through and then it's back to my side to hang up the staff on the 'bull-horn' at the end of the platform. My driver opens the regulator and without even thinking about it, I lean forward from my seat to pull on the chain and lift the flap up to cover the firehole, to prevent too much cold air entering the firebox.

Down around the Coombe viaduct we run by the side of the Lynher River to Wearde. A quick glance over the side and I can see the line of the former Cornwall Railway branching off as a siding. Time to go to work again as we run towards Shillingham Tunnel and St Germans. A glance in the box tells me what needs to be done, so I begin to feed the coal to the places where it is most needed. A few shovelfuls up the front and especially in the corners, and then in the back corners. Nothing drastic now, but after the tunnel the gradient will increase in severity, and a little preparation now will help for the harder work to come. I see my mate look across and give a small nod

acknowledging that all is well; the boiler shows water just below the top of the glass, and the steam gauge pointer steady on the red line.

Through St Germans and some serious 'collar work' is called for. The reversing lever is gradually allowed to ease forward permitting a longer stroke to the pistons, as we roar under the road bridge and face the couple of miles of 1 in 70 to Trerule Foot before easing out to Menheniot. Steady work now on the footplate, as both sides concentrate on their respective tasks. The track levels out before Menheniot, with slight section of falling gradient, but then as we go through the station the regulator opens again for the pull up to Cartuther before falling once more on the approaches to Liskeard, where we have a station stop. I have always felt that that section of track upon leaving the Royal Albert Bridge epitomises the Cornish Road.

There are steeper gradients ahead but the basic work on the footplate is the same; an awareness of steam and boiler control. Best practice meant getting the best results from every pound of coal and each gallon of water. Both should be used to the fullest extent but neither should be wasted. The blowing off through the safety valves of excess steam as well as being a nuisance to any one in the vicinity, was considered to be a waste, and proper management of the level of water in the boiler could

1962 and the road bridge had been constructed. I accept that it offers untold advantage in getting into 'England', but is in no way as interesting either as a steam ferry or even a steam train! It has however formed an advantageous site for the many railway photographers when a steam-hauled 'special' crosses the Royal Albert Bridge.

A second, much older, vantage point favoured by photographers is Lower Fore Street in Saltash. It is possible to obtain nicely framed 'shots' of a train either entering or departing through the western portal, or on the land spans. The white building lower centre with the pedestrians walking past was demolished in a local housing clearance and improvement scheme in the late 1960s, and is now where the author lives. It affords excellent views of trains crossing, you will not be surprised to learn!

On 14 April 1952 newly painted 6801 AYLBURTON GRANGE, in British Railways black with red lining, is approaching Coombe by Saltash viaduct with the 3.15pm down stopping passenger train. The Granges performed well and were popular over the Cornish Road. R.E. Vincent, www.transporttreasury.co.uk

Liskeard west end on 2 October 1954 and plenty of steam to spare. Excessive 'blowing-off' of steam from the safety valve was frowned upon by some footplate inspectors, as bad boiler management by the fireman. It was regarded as a waste of coal and water. At times, however, and with a freely steaming locomotive, such things were unavoidable. The up passenger train on the main line is headed by Grange 4-6-0, well known for their steaming qualities. The pannier tank off the trip goods and shunting the shed and sidings joins in the act. R.E. Vincent, www.transporttreasury.co.uk

Bodmin Road station and the distinctive water column on the up side. With the tank strategically located to gather water from the River Fowey below, the gantry gave access to the main line without the need to install pipes beneath the two sets of track. James Harrold, www.transporttreasury.co.uk

The west end at Bodmin Road and Laira's large prairie 5148, working a trip goods from Tavistock Junction to St Austell is running around her train on the up main line. In the cloud of steam a stopping passenger service is ready to depart the down platform.

After the long run down Largin bank from Doublebois Laira's 5972 OLTON HALL coasts through Bodmin Road with a partially fitted goods train. The fireman will be aware of the damage caused to his fire on the long downhill section, and will steadily build it up once again before Lostwithiel for the climb up to Treverrin. R.E. Vincent, www.transporttreasury.co.uk

1007 COUNTY OF BRECKNOCK re-starts the up Falmouth-Paddington away from Par, after collecting the coaches from the Newquay branch passenger, 11 July 1956. S. Creer, www.transporttreasury.co.uk

St Austell station, looking westward from the road bridge. The sidings to the right later became the terminus for the Motor-Rail link, but is now inevitably a car park. The Great Western Railway Staff Association Social Club stands at the west end. I used to daily cross over the footbridge at the west end on the way to and from School. N. Simmons.

St Austell in 1911, looking east along Fore Street. Towering above all at the far end is Trinity Church, where the author rang the bells in May 1939 for a Special Festival, at the age of nine years. As will be seen from the image, the young men and boys of St Austell readily posed for photographs whenever a camera was present. Mr Hodge, the proprietor of the shop on the left, was a nursery seedsman, but was also the proprietor of the Sun Inn at Market Street, opposite to the Church.

obviate that. It was not always possible to achieve the perfect situation of course, but the Cornish and Devon roads with their 'up hill and down dale' nature were perfect in fact for developing this expertise it was evolve or die! It was called 'knowing the road'. Whereas a driver signed to state that he was competent to drive a train over a section of line, so a fireman *learnt* the road, being able to judge how far a boiler of water would take him up a bank before having to put the feed on. It was especially important when having a rough trip and struggling to coach steam out of a reluctant locomotive. It was imperative to know just when the regulator would be closed and for how long; when to let the water level drop for a couple of miles prior so that on the down hill section you could put cold water into a hot boiler and cool it down, thereby not blowing off.

Leaving Liskeard for Doublebois with a passenger train presents no undue problems, for all the carriages have a continuous brake and are close coupled. The fireman's thoughts are with the long falling section ahead from Doublebois to Bodmin Road and Lostwithiel, and he will not be concerned at placing water back into the boiler, for this can be done going down that bank. With a goods train however, the situation is different. From Liskeard there is an immediate fall of 1 in 60 towards Moorswater viaduct and a rising gradient immediately thereafter. With a partially vacuum-fitted train all will

be well as long as the regulator is opened and the forward movement sufficient to keep the couplings taut.

With a loose coupled train care has to be taken to ensure that the couplings are kept taut, avoiding a sudden 'snatch' of the back end of the train snapping a coupling and thus dividing the train – a disaster. The guard usually assists with judicious and prudent use of the handbrake in his van. All goes well and as you run over the viaduct the height is unnervingly apparent. Up now towards Doublebois, and the fireman will be putting coal on the back end of the fire to ensure that by Bodmin Road and Lostwithiel, after the long run down the Largin bank, there will still be a good 'body' of fire to build upon for the eventual climb from Lostwithiel to Treverrin tunnel on the way to Par.

On a passenger train, over the top at Doublebois (the translation is 'Two Woods') and with the cut-off on the reversing lever in the 'drift' at about 35%, the driver uses the vacuum brake with great skill to hold the speed of the train back to the regulation 45 mph. The fireman has a chance to once again 'tidy up' the footplate and damp down the front edge and the coal in the tender, before sitting down to enjoy the view of the wooded valley. It was a different story entirely for the crew of a goods train; none of the wagons, or perhaps only a small number of them are vacuum fitted and

trouble-free operation requires the utmost attention and concentration. The overall falling gradient is still a bit like the teeth on a saw; sections of 1 in 80 or thereabouts steepen to 1 in 60 at the 250 milepost and there are short, almost unnoticeable 'hiccups' of level or adverse gradient. The fireman would be assisting with the braking by careful adjustment of the tender handbrake, as would the guard, unseen at the rear of the train in his van.

There is a levelling out on the approach to Bodmin Road station before dropping sharply once again at 1 in 70 to the tunnel at Brown Queen. A gradual easing from here gives some degree of respite from the continual concentration as the station at Lostwithiel marks the end of the falling gradient. The next section is uphill, to the tunnel at Treverrin. There are no easy ways to tackle this rising two miles of 1 in 70/80, with a final 1 in 65 to the mouth of the tunnel. It is hard work for the fireman. He needs firstly to repair the ravages done to the fire on that long downhill section, though he knows that he can 'play' the boiler for once through the tunnel when the gradient falls once more to Par.

The difficulty is that from Par it is all pulling ground yet again, up through St Austell to Burngullow, some eight miles ahead. If the crew get a chance they can glimpse the exceptional scenery, the wide expanse of St Austell Bay opening up on

Truro station in July 1956 and 4-6-0 6835 EASTHAM GRANGE from Bristol Bath Road shed is waiting for signals before re-starting the 2.0pm Penzance to Crewe parcels train. To permit station duties, this train was booked to stop at Truro for 15 minutes. S. Creer, www.transporttreasury.co.uk

On 11 May 1959 local engine 6875 HINDFORD GRANGE is passing the engine shed at 'Long Rock' with the 1.55pm up stopping passenger service to Plymouth. To the left is the sea with, if we could but see them, its prominent offshore rocks. Michael Mensing.

An immaculate 1007 COUNTY OF BRECKNOCK runs in to Penzance with the 4.25pm Truro to Penzance stopping train. H.C. Casserley, courtesy R.M. Casserley.

the fireman's side. The driver makes do with the white man-made mountains of clay waste that herald the clay country. The line is level through the major clay works at Burngullow, where the mineral line to St Dennis Junction on the Par-Newquay line branches away northwards. Then comes another long down gradient, to Probus and Ladock Platform, interrupted by a short uphill section before Grampound Road. This again calls for careful use of the brakes on a goods train if a 'snatch' at the change of gradient about half-way is not to thoroughly ruin everyone's day. From Probus and Ladock there are just a couple more 'hiccups' through the tunnels at Polprerro and Budshead before catching sight of Cornwall's only city. Its beautiful three-spire cathedral heralds the approach of the station at Truro. A goods train might have reason to call at the goods yard but otherwise locomotives, whether on a goods or passenger, will stop by the water column at the west end of the down platform, to replenish the tender for the final run to Penzance.

The crew of the goods train would probably be relieved here, so the fireman would have been busy in the tender after the tunnels, to get some coal forward. He would also make sure that the boiler was full and a full head of steam present to give his relief a head start. The fireman on a passenger train for Penzance would also be ensuring all was ship-shape, but for his own benefit, and would get some coal forward in the station whilst the tender was filling with water. Both drivers would be having a check around the locomotive, feeling that all was running cool and topping up the oil wells. By the time for 'right away', hopefully the safety valves would have lifted, and the climb

out of Truro and up to the tunnel at Highertown was underway.

The driver would have a good view of the shed at Truro, tucked into the corner as it were against the high ground surrounding the tunnel. His mate, of course would again be 'head down' in the time-honoured way, striving to maintain a full head of steam. Once through the tunnel Penwithers Junction opens out with the branch line to Falmouth and the mineral line to Newham Wharves leaving the main line on the down side. Three more miles or so of rising 1 in 80 follow before a levelling out at Chacewater. The countryside is different now, the fields giving way to Cornwall's scarred ancient mining areas. It is 1 in 70 most of the way and the regulator will be on the second valve, and the reversing lever dropping forward snick by snick to lengthen the stroke of the pistons. This will not be appreciated by the fireman, however, for it would mean a heavier demand on his side of the footplate. Anyone watching and listening would be wholly unaware of this of course, and would instead doubtless take joy in the regular beat of the exhaust, a music that only Great Western locomotives could summon up.

There is a short fall down to Chacewater before pulling again up to Scorrier for the start of the highest section in West Cornwall. Decision time for the fireman. A Penzance man with a Penzance locomotive will be giving thought to working the fire down for the disposal procedures at Penzance shed. A Laira man on the other hand, with a Laira engine, will be aware that he has the best part of a couple of hours at Penzance before the return so will want to preserve the fire. This will give him a good start on the

return but he will not want to have too much of a hot fire in the box, with the chance of unwanted 'blowing of' during the stay.

A goods train for Penzance would be bound for the sidings at Marazion in all probability, thereafter to run light engine to the shed. For the passenger train there is another fifteen miles or so yet, and relaxation is not yet an option. From just before Camborne the gradient again changes, falling for five or so miles and another true Cornish 'hiccup' is encountered, the hump at St Erth. After that comes a leisurely run past Marazion and its yards to Mounts Bay with St Michael's Mount dominating all, before coming to a stop in the platform at Penzance. For a Penzance crew all that was left was to let the passengers depart before setting back with the coaches to the sidings. After that it was a light run to Penzance (locally called 'Long Rock' shed) for booking off. For the Laira men it was the same procedure except the 'booking off' part. Their loco would have to turn and perhaps take coal while they grabbed a bite to eat and a can of tea before checking over the loco again; oiling, sanding, all the rest. Then, it was a case of doing it all again, in reverse.

****

Laira shed of course lay in Devon, *in England* no less, but it played both a supporting and central part (if that makes sense) in the work of the Cornish sheds. The Cornish sheds 'owned' the majority of the work in the county but the main line Plymouth-Penzance, the spine as it were, was to an extent shared between the 'native' sheds and Laira. In this way the latter's men and locomotives made

Truro station on 30 May 1960. L.R. Freeman, www.transporttreasury.co.uk

Redruth, looking east on 30 May 1960. The white twin-gabled building beyond, nestling under the slope to the right of the down platform, is the railway social club. Cornish and Plymouth retired steam men still meet there. L.R. Freeman, www.transporttreasury.co.uk

Gwinear Road, from the country end, 30 May 1960. L.R. Freeman, www.transporttreasury.co.uk

their own contribution to the life of the Duchy.

Generally, all goods trains worked by Cornish crews out of the county to the east terminated at Tavistock Junction. They were either relieved there by Laira men and took another goods back with a turned and readied engine, or went with their original engine light to the shed for turning before working another train back over the Royal Albert Bridge and on into Cornwall. Normal 'everyday' trains would be remarshalled and their loadings adjusted for onward passage over the Devon road. These trains were worked forward to Newton Abbot or Exeter by a Laira footplate crew or perhaps a Newton crew working back home.

The seasonal traffics, broccoli and new potatoes were regarded as 'semi-fast' and under normal circumstances such a train, from Cornwall, would terminate at Tavistock Junction and a fresh crew and engine out of Laira would be waiting to work forward. Occasionally a 'foreign' locomotive from perhaps Exeter or Taunton shed would be working back home and the change-over of crews could be done on the main line, opposite Laira shed at Lipson Junction.

St Blazey had charge of the clay branch workings but as with everything else the clay trains came into Laira's orbit once they crossed the Royal Albert Bridge. Laira crews and locos worked the clay trains forward, as they did everything else and we were well aware of the problems of train control on these heavy trains where the wagons had 'loose' couplings. This fashion of working possibly rendered Cornwall unique in that its locos scarcely ventured far beyond the county boundary. Tavistock Junction for goods engines was an invisible barrier; passenger engines out of Cornwall tended to come off at North Road. They might run a little

further east, to Laira, for servicing but this could also be done using the triangle and sidings to the *west* of North Road, at the Cornwall end of the station. This triangle was formed of the Cornish main line, the line to Millbay and the section from Cornwall Junction to the Cornish line. Inside the three lines were a couple of sidings, an inspection pit and a turntable. The place served much as Ranelagh Bridge did at Paddington, to 'quicken' engine turnrounds without occupying tracks in time-consuming runs to Laira. At times, it could be congested and if the case was that an engine just required to be turned the signalman sent it 'round the angle'.

At one time there had been clay quarrying in the Plymouth area too, and on the north-eastern outskirts of the city there existed what was reputed to be the largest clay pit in existence. This was on the southern slopes of Dartmoor at Lee Moor where, in the mid-1920s, the workings covered an area of forty acres, excavated to a depth of some 150 feet. It was not served directly by the Great Western but instead the whole output of this giant undertaking was carried on a 4ft 6in gauge tramway *worked by horses*. It ran down from Lee Moor and crossed the Great Western main line at Laira Junction on the level, on its way to the wharves at Cattedown.

Lee Moor clay was sent the Potteries in Staffordshire and ran on our lines to the ports of Fowey and Par. I recall working the morning goods to Tavistock and on the return journey calling at Marsh Mills to collect wagons of clay which we took Laira yard. I believe that the up side shunting engine at the Junction would also run into Marsh Mills for the same purpose.

I always liked to work trains of 'cattle empties' back down to Drump Lane for distribution onwards to the various

country yards where their occupants would be driven for their last journey. With vacuum brakes (usually on the first third of the train) braking was no longer such a problem, and it was almost like working a passenger train. Apart from the need to retire into a loop while a following passenger train went by, we did not stop.

It really didn't matter, of course, whether Laira, St Blazey, Truro or Penzance engines and men were working a given train. To a crew it was just another day, and in the case of the 'specials', we had a booked turn, and thus infinitely preferable to simply waiting in the enginemens cabin for something to crop up. I often reflect that we were barely interested in the precise type of train. We would of course be aware of loading, brakes and so on; that some trains were going to be heavier than others, some would have vacuum brakes and that others would require the guard to come forward to pin down handbrakes on the leading wagons at the top of the banks. Any fireman's thoughts (like mine) were more likely to have been directed towards the locomotive and its condition, and to how it would perform. Would she be free steaming, or would it turn out to be a struggle between me and 'her'?

1006 COUNTY OF CORNWALL on the 1.55pm ex-Penzance coming into Gwinear Road on 30 May 1960. At the east end were a number of sidings for the broccoli traffic. L.R. Freeman, www.transporttreasury.co.uk

A poorly turned out 6863 DOLHYWELL GRANGE (not the usual standard for a Laira loco on passenger work) with the 5.50pm Penzance-Truro, arriving at St Erth on 30 May 1960. L.R. Freeman, www.transporttreasury.co.uk

Liskeard main platforms, looking east on 31 May 1960. The crossover at the end of the platforms leads to the goods yard and the Looe branch L.R. Freeman, www.transporttreasury.co.uk

5972 OLTON HALL approaching Gwinear Road, 18 August 1958. A.E. Bennett, www.transporttreasury.co.uk

A lifelong enthusiasm is born (we hope!) at Penzance station, courtesy 6931 ALDBOROUGH HALL on the 6.45 p.m. train for Plymouth, 17 August 1958. A.E. Bennett, www.transporttreasury.co.uk

End of the line. On 19 May 1959 4955 PLASPOWER HALL simmers quietly in the station at Penzance after bringing in the 7.35am stopping passenger service from Newton Abbot. Michael Mensing.

Towan Beach, Newquay with Bishop Rock extreme left. Rising above the headland and the beach is the former Great Western Hotel.

Small prairie 5526 at Middle Way crossing, St Blazey with a branch passenger train for Newquay. R.C. Riley, www.transporttreasury.co.uk

Chapter 5
Of Branches and Engine Sheds: St Blazey

Newquay was linked to the main line through Cornwall in three separate ways.

1. From Par station. A line, almost 21 miles long, opened fully in the mid-1880s, taking in the former Treffry, Newquay and Cornwall Minerals Railways through the Luxulyan Valley, and across the Goss Moors to Bugle, St Dennis Junction and on to Newquay. The line was taken over in 1896 when the Great Western purchased the Cornwall Minerals Railway in its entirety.

2. From Burngullow, on the main Cornish Road two miles west of St Austell. A seven mile mineral line running directly northwards was constructed in 1869 by the Newquay and Cornwall Junction Railway, its purpose to serve six main groups of china clay sidings as well as a major complex at Drinnick Mill. It was then intended to extend it to join the Par to Newquay Branch line at St Dennis Junction. The NCJR ran into financial difficulties and the section from Drinnick to St Dennis Junction was completed by the Cornwall Minerals Railway. From October 1877 the line was worked by the Great Western Railway until as in (1) above it was included in the takeover of the CMR.

3. From Chacewater. A line, almost nineteen miles in length, was opened in two stages by the Great Western and completed in 1905. It connected the main line west of Truro with St Agnes and Perranporth, eventually joining the Par-Newquay line at Tolcarn Junction a mile east of Newquay.

The lines (1 and 2) from Par and Burngullow were the province of St Blazey shed, though in BR days Laira crews worked certain through passenger trains. The line from Chacewater was worked by Truro locomotives and crews.

Par-Newquay
Next to the resorts in South Devon, Newquay was perhaps the principal holiday destination in the West Country. The Par to Newquay line was very busy in the summer season, with passenger trains from the north of England and London added to the normal weekday service. On the Saturday this already busy schedule was further stretched to include the 'Special' trains ran to cater for the needs of the holiday trade. I have already mentioned the need for additional locomotive power but the powers-that-be in their wisdom laid down a stipulation as to who was responsible for the coupling

and uncoupling. On Mondays to Fridays, a through train would be stopped at St Blazey advanced starting signal, and the Shunter from St Blazey Yard would couple up the assisting locomotive to the front of the train engine. The uncoupling at either Luxulyan (top of the incline) or at Tolcarne Junction (prior to entering Newquay Station) would be the responsibility of the fireman of the leading locomotive.

On Saturdays the assisting locomotive was attached at Par Station and the responsibility for coupling up and uncoupling was vested with the fireman of the assisting locomotive. The collection of the Single Line Working Token was the responsibility of the fireman of the train engine. Congestion became acute at the Newquay end of the line where, from Tolcarne Junction the section to the station at Newquay also had to cater for the trains from Truro and Penzance via Chacewater (see Chapter 7) which connected at that point. At the height of the season on a summer Saturday there could be as many as twenty trains each way on the Par-Newquay line with a further twelve each way to Chacewater.

There was always an imbalance of the number of inward trains compared to the

Newquay on 26 July 1958. Laira's 7909 HEVENINGHAM HALL is standing in the station awaiting 'right away' with a stopping passenger train for Plymouth North Road. Terry Nicholls.

outward ones on the Par to Newquay line due to some extent by the limitation on loading for the Luxulyan bank for trains working in the direction of Newquay.

Par dep.	Newquay arr.	Originated from
04.50	05.50	19.15 ex Sheffield
05.10	06.10	22.50 ex Paddington
06.10	07.05	Local
06.55	07.49	21.50 ex Wolverhampton
07.45	08.49	Local
08.10	09.25	21.15 ex Manchester.
09.22	10.31	Local
10.05	10.58	Local
10.48	11.45	Local
12.25	13.29	Local
13.38	14.40	Local
14.07	15.00	Local
14.40	15.42	Local
15.15	16.05	Local
15.27	16.30	09.30 ex Paddington
17.30	18.32	Local
18.12	19.15	Local
18.54	19.50	13.45 ex Bristol
19.30	20.32	Local
20.00	21.13	13.35 ex Paddington
21.20	22.12	Local

Newquay dep.	Par arr.	Destination
07.50	08.41	Manchester
08.05	09.03	Newcastle
08.52	09.52	Local
10.00	11.00	Paddington
11.00	11.46	York
11.15	12.09	Wolverhampton
11.53	12.52	Local
12.30	13.14	Paddington
12.42	13.40	Cardiff
12.50	13.45	Local
13.45	14.42	Paddington
14.00	14.50	Local
15.10	16.10	Local
17.00	18.00	Local
18.00	18.56	Plymouth
20.00	20.55	Local
21.07	22.06	Local
22.15	23.11	Local

Normal branch trains were made up of two-four carriages behind a 45XX 'small prairie' 2-6-2T, occasionally supplemented by a 57XX pannier tank and a couple of carriages. The through trains, of course, could bring any manner of tender engines, except for the Kings which were prohibited west of Keyham, Devonport.

Passenger traffic aside, the line's main purpose was to carry china clay, to the ports of Newquay early on, then Par and Fowey. The working of clay trains over the various branches and spurs which extended from the through line was most difficult because of the nature of the terrain. Severe inclines and falling gradients often demanded banking locomotives one moment, and the pinning down by hand of the brakes on the clay wagons the next. Rails and handbrakes would become slimy and slippery with clay in the wet, and clouds of white dust would billow up in the dry times, the ultra-fine material penetrating everywhere.

The work called for the best expertise from footplate crews, guards and shunters alike, and with all due respect to the men of the other Cornish sheds it is perhaps true to state that for this class of work, there were none more adept at it than those from St Blazey.

Bodmin
An outstation of St Blazey for engines working the Bodmin Road to Bodmin and Wadebridge branches, it was a single road stone built shed which housed two 'small prairie' 2-6-2Ts of the 45XX series. 4508 and 4552 for instance were there at one time in the 1950s. The original Bodmin to Wadebridge Railway, opened in July 1834, was

reputedly Cornwall's first line to make use of locomotives. It was extended in September 1834, from Boscarne Junction to Wenford for the clay works at De Lank Quarries, taking the stuff to the port of Padstow. The London & South Western Railway, having taken the North Cornwall line to Halwill, extended to Padstow and took over this new section. The clay was worked by South Western 2-4-0 well tanks and an extension to Dunmere was made. The LSWR's station was called Bodmin North. Padstow and Wadebridge to Bodmin North became the 'main' line with the six miles Boscarne Junction-Wenford becoming the 'branch'.

The Great Western opened its branch from Bodmin Road on the main line to Bodmin and had a separate station called Bodmin General. With Fowey fast developing as a port, the GW extended to the LSWR at Boscarne Junction and Wenford clay wagons began to be taken out to Lostwithiel and Fowey; GW passenger trains ran to Wadebridge on the LSWR, making this corner of Cornwall a den of politicking and rivalry between the companies. All this lived on until the closures of the 1960s, in a friendly daily bantering accompanied by a steadfast though tongue in cheek refusal to admit any good in the other's practices. The 2½

Bugle Station, 28 April 1962; D6323 With a Par-Newquay train is passing a Plymouth Railway Circle brake van tour hauled by prairie tanks 4564 and 5531. The photographer (a former Railway Clerk) had used his connections to have the engines coupled bunker to bunker to ensure that whichever way they travelled there would be a chimney leading! Terry Nicholls.

mile, 1 in 40 descent to Bodmin Road with a fully laden clay train required the putting down of brakes on the leading wagons, and a restriction of twenty miles per hour was in force. Similar restrictions applied to the three mile stretch also falling at 1 in 40, from Bodmin General to Boscarne, and on the Wenford branch for all of its seven mile plunge to Boscarne Junction. These gradients brought out the best in all footplate crews no matter where their loyalties lay.

Top. **On 24 July 1958 4294, one of St Blazey's two 2-8-0Ts (fairly uncommon away from their native heath in South Wales) crosses the public footpath leading to Par Beach with empty clay wagons from Fowey to St Blazey yard. The young lady watching the train as she waits to use the footpath is a Miss Margaret Richardson of Saltash. Terry Nicholls.**

Middle. **St Blazey's 42XX 2-8-0T 4247 at Par Sands on 18 April 1955, heading for St Blazey yard with a train of empty clay wagons. Brian C. Bailey.**

Below. **East end of Par station. A local goods train, possibly from Burngullow, has arrived on the up main line behind an 0-6-0PT and is ready to reverse on to the branch line to proceed to St Blazey goods yard. So that the pannier does not have to uncouple and run around the train, and then switch the brake to the other end, small prairie 5537 has coupled to the rear of the train and will lead the whole ensemble back to St Blazey. S. Creer, www.transporttreasury.co.uk**

Top. St Blazey tanks 5521 and 3635 approach Par with an up train of 'sheeted down' clay wagons, probably destined for the docks, 6 July 1955. R.C. Riley, www.transporttreasury.co.uk

Middle. The west end of Par station, 11 July 1956 and Penzance 4-6-0 6806 BLACKWELL GRANGE re-starts the Falmouth portion of the 9.30am ex-Paddington, at the commencement of the long climb up to St Austell. S. Creer, www.transporttreasury.co.uk

Below. St Blazey's 4565 standing in the branch platform at Bodmin Road with a two coach train for Bodmin General.

Bodmin Road branch platform, 4 June 1960. The crew of 2-6-2T 4569 are waiting for the parcels to be loaded on to the train before it can depart for Bodmin General. James Harrold, www.transporttreasury.co.uk

Bodmin General on 4 June 1960 and 4569 has arrived; after reversing the carriages clear of the crossover, it has uncoupled and pulled ahead ready to run around the train. James Harrold, www.transporttreasury.co.uk

Top. 4552 plus a brake van, in the up sidings at Bodmin Road station on 4 June 1960. In all probability it has worked a clay train from Boscarne Junction destined for Par, and is in the process of changing ends with the van. James Harrold, www.transporttreasury.co.uk

Middle. On 4 June 1960 a train of empty clay wagons hauled by pannier tank 7709 is standing on the up road at Bodmin Road. A westbound passenger train is at the down platform. The wagons have probably come from Carne Point in the Fowey estuary via Lostwithiel, and are destined to go up the Bodmin branch for the Wenford Bridge line. When the passenger has departed 7709 will run around the train and then proceed up the branch line. James Harrold, www.transporttreasury.co.uk

Below. 4666 standing in Bodmin North station at the head of the 11.20am local service for Wadebridge. The Southern men were inclined to affect indifference when asked to expound upon the merits of a Western locomotive. James Harrold, www.transporttreasury.co.uk

Small prairie 5573 with clay wagons at Bodmin General; beyond is the little one road engine shed. R.C. Riley, www.transporttreasury.co.uk

Moorswater Shed

A curious outpost with its origins in the old Liskeard and Caradon Railway, it housed a pair of the 'small prairies'. It was oddly famous for its loo, a 'cludgie' formed from a locomotive firebox. It can safely be said that this was the most photographed engine shed toilet in the world. Occupants sat on sleepers arranged over the stream; a newspaper was vital, and not just for reading. The 2-6-2Ts for the mineral work and the branch passenger trains Liskeard-Looe (thirty trains on a peak summer day) came from St Blazey.

St Blazey Shed and Workings

The engine shed at St Blazey lay in the heart of the clay country, so naturally the main preoccupation, in addition to normal main and branch duties, was the serving of the clay quarries. It is not my intention to write of the history of clay mining and the St Austell area, this has already been done by much more competent and knowledgeable persons. Although Par had been developed for clay exports since 1820, Fowey became the principal port for the china clay by the 1870s. It was first connected by rail via Lostwithiel, and then in 1874 to Par through the celebrated Pinnock tunnel burrowed under the Great Pinnock Hill. Centred around Carne Point the complex was eventually to have eight jetties and numerous quays for the loading of clay into ships. At the height of its activities it is said to have been loading some 1½ million tons of clay a year. Smaller amounts were shipped from

the docks at Charlestown and Pentewan. Almost invariably the clay went from pit to dockside by rail, in hooded wooden four wheeled wagons. Charlestown Harbour did not have a rail connection and in my boyhood it was still possible to see horses hauling ancient wagons of clay there.

The shed was unusual in its layout, and there could have been few like it in Britain. A sort of semi-circle, it had six roads 70 feet long, three either side of three central roads which extended into the repair shops. Two of these roads were over 100 feet long. Operating instructions for shunting the shop and workshop sidings were that 'all wagons should be connected to the locomotive and not uncoupled until brought to a stand and properly secured.' The 55½ft turntable was vacuum operated, with connections off it to the coal stage, workshops and the through road for St Blazey Junction to the west and Par and Fowey to the east. Regrettably it has not been possible to obtain Link Workings or Rosters for the St. Blazey shed, but I am grateful to those who have supplied the following information.

In 1950 the staff and their locos were as follows, so far as I can ascertain…
Head Foreman/Shed Master: Bill Coe
Shed Clerk: Raymond Snell.
Shift Foreman/Chargehands: ? Dunn, Fred Bishop, Fred Northam, George Thomas (formerly of Laira).
Drivers: Sid Coe; ? Gill; Carey Batchelor; Jeff Kimber; Bill Rundle; ? Osborne, Joe Preston; Ike Fuge and others.
Firemen: Barry Sullivan, Geoff Kimber,

Jack Hooper, John Shepland and others
4-6-0: 4940 LUDFORD HALL, 5926 GROTRIAN HALL
2-6-0: 6330, 6356
2-8-0T: 4215, 4298
2-6-2T: 4503, 4505, 4516, 4529, 4552, 4559, 4570, 5519, 5531; 5158
0-6-0PT: 1900, 1930, 2050, 2181, 2182, 2780, 6420, 7709, 7715, 8783, 9656

Train Movements - St. Blazey
Goods Yard 1955

St Austell china clay came mainly from five branch mineral lines.
1. The Retew branch, a 4 mile 2 chain line south from the Newquay branch at St Dennis Junction to Melangoose Sidings, extended to Meledor Sidings.

2. Burngullow branch; 4 mile 46 chain line south from St Dennis Junction extending via Drinnick Mill to the St Austell-Truro main line at Burngullow.

3. Carbis branch, a short line running westwards from the Newquay line at Bugle, serving Carbis and Wheal Rose.

4. Goonbarrow branch, a 1 mile 60 chain line from the Newquay line south of Bugle serving the Caudledown and Carbean areas.

5. The Trenance Valley branch, known to railwaymen as 'Bojea', a 1 mile 35 chain line from the St Austell-Truro main line just west of St Austell, at Trenance Siding, extending northwards to the Carlyon Kiln sidings near Trethowel, Bojea Yard, Lower

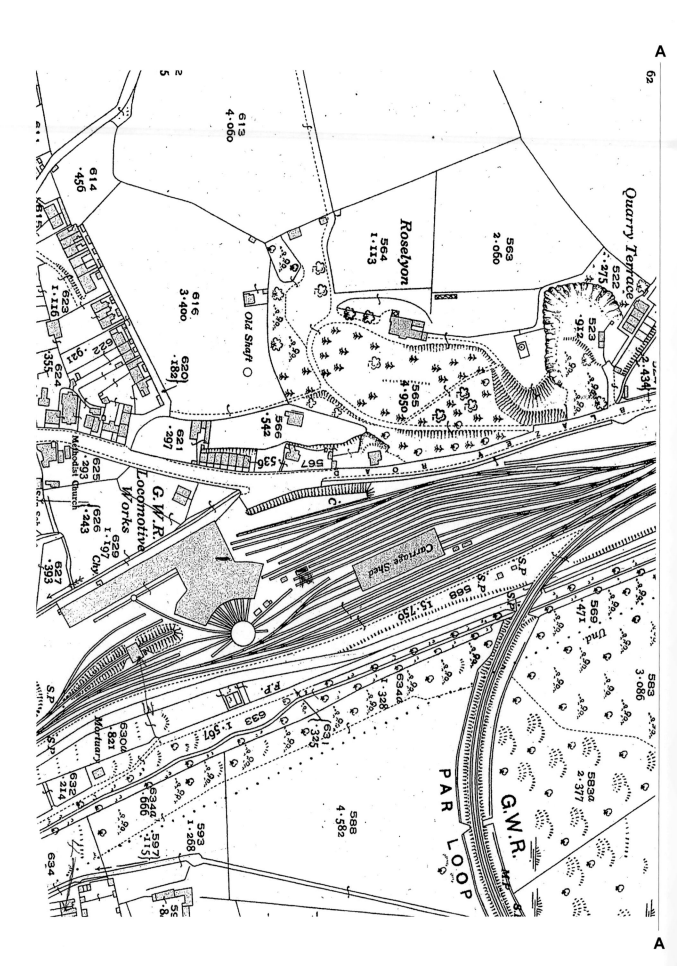

A

B

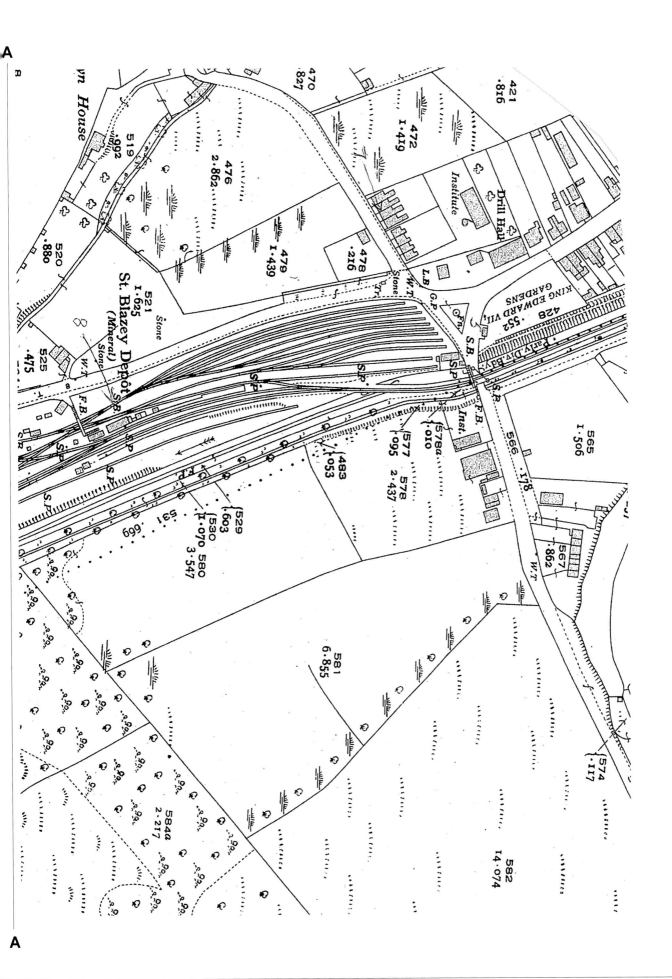

A

Bodmin General from the platform end looking from the area of the signal box (the engine shed is further behind us). This is now the home of course of the preserved Bodmin & Wenford Railway. James Harrold, www.transporttreasury.co.uk

A view north from the St Blazey shed and works to the old station and beyond. Track on the right through the disused platforms with the tell-tale shine on the rails is the Par to Newquay branch through this former Cornwall Railways station. It was closed in the mid-1920s but the signal box remained in use. The right-hand track was the 'main' used by all through trains. The left-hand platform line is the access to some of the goods and works sidings. The 'up' platform has the signal post and the 'bull horn' post and arm for the setting down of the staff, the line from here eastwards being single track. The wisp of smoke in the centre background indicates a pannier tank shunting the goods sidings. R.C. Riley, www.transporttreasury.co.uk

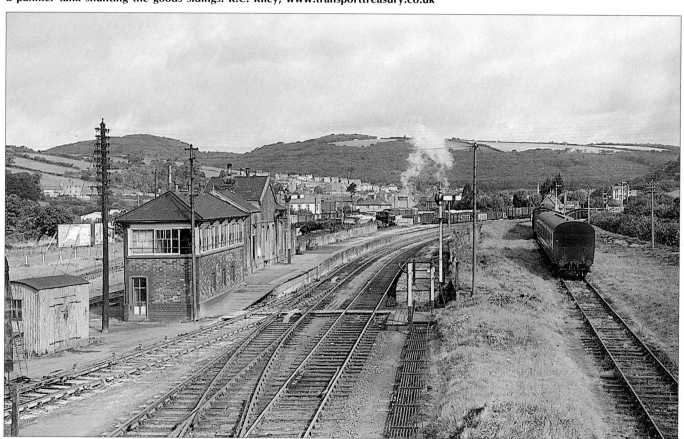

St Blazey shed, from Par Harbour Signal Box, 2 September 1954. In front is the 'pick up & set down' post for the single line working staff. The western end of the shed and coal stage can be seen behind the signal gantry, with the workshop complex left. A 45XX prairie tank is collecting coal wagons from the sidings to replenish the coal stage. R.C. Riley, www.transporttreasury.co.uk

Ruddle wharf and Lansalson wharf at Ruddlemoor.

In Chapter Two of *Laira Fireman* I recounted a story of the exploits of the Cleaner Boys at the St Blazey shed, the concocting of a 'suicide' at Five Arches. I also intimated that my older brother who did his cleaning days at the shed was probably a party to that escapade. I have since found out that my suspicions was correct and later in this Chapter I include a couple more stories of their 'high jinks'. The following story is however of the first firing turns, so eagerly looked forward to by the young cleaners including, of course, myself.

As the occasion arose; holidays, sickness or the increased demands of additional trains for the summer season, senior cleaner boys would receive an internal temporary promotion to the footplate grades. Senior fireman who had passed their exams were promoted to temporary drivers, and accordingly a similar number of senior cleaners were made temporary firemen. For cleaners this was the ultimate goal - *firing turns upon the footplate at last!* For a cleaner boy of course, this first firing turn, and indeed all of them, were the realisation of a dream and no matter what, a pannier tank was a King for that shift. This would carry on until the end of the summer season, when the majority of those temporarily promoted would suffer a return to the status quo. The brief footplate freedom came to an end and it was back to cleaning.

I well recall my first firing turn as cleaner boy. I was paired with a driver called Les Plummer, and rostered to shunt the down sidings at the Tavistock Junction marshalling yard at Marsh Mills. I recall that I kept wanting to shovel coal into the firebox, after all wasn't that that a fireman did? until Les, in desperation, and in no uncertain manner told me to sit down and only pick the shovel up when he told me to.

Brother Bill had a most spectacular first turn, paired with a driver called Beckerleg, though neither he nor any of the surviving St Blazey men can recall his Christian name. They had charge of the shunting engine for the clay sidings at Carne Point Jetties, on the Fowey River estuary. The place was notable not least for a general labourer, and celebrated character, with the peculiar nickname of 'Titty-Fo-La' though sadly no one knew why. It turned out he was grandfather to Donald Tabb, a fellow engine cleaner on Bill's shift. Donald's father, Titty-Fo-La's son, had a smallholding on which he grew apple trees and made his own cider, and the said TFL it seems, had a liking for this powerful stuff. He could regularly be seen taking a swig of it from an ever-present bottle. He reputedly drank two pints of it every morning to wash down his breakfast. It was a matter of some comment that the copious amounts drank had little or no effect upon the manner in which he carried out his work.

The Great Western/Western Region lines in Devon and Cornwall were organised for operating purposes as the

Newton Abbot Division and the shed there, with its extensive works, was the 'HQ' of the division as it were. We at Laira barely recognised this, for wasn't Plymouth a great city and port and Newton Abbot some anonymous village on Dartmoor? Needless to say Laira was without doubt (in our minds) vastly senior to the hopelessly parochial Cornish sheds. Did we not have the prestigious double home turns to London, crewing the magnificent Kings which were too grand even to enter Cornwall, and we had the uniquely difficult South Devon Banks. The crews at St Blazey were painfully aware of our condescending attitude but it really wasn't much more than carefully contrived humour and work in Cornwall was anything but easy and parochial. St Blazey for instance had a couple of fearsome inclines to deal with and one in particular (though we'd never admit it) was possibly more daunting than anything in Devon.

The severe 1 in 37 and 1 in 40 gradients of the Luxulyan bank on the Newquay branch, rising some 600 feet to the summit at Roche, presented a challenge every bit the equal of Dainton or Rattery and was comparable in every way to the work of the Laira men over the South Devon lines. The severity of Luxulyan meant that not only did the majority of trains, goods and passenger alike required the assistance of a banker at the rear; the heavily laden passenger trains in the summer would also need an additional locomotive *on the front*. I describe the working of a through London to Newquay express passenger

The 'back' of St Blazey shed on 10 December 1958. The sidings are full of loco coal ready for the coal stage on the raised incline. To the left can be seen the impressive buildings which housed the Workshops and Engineering Departments.

train over this bank in Chapter Four of *Laira Fireman*. It only needs me to add that the working of any class of train on that stretch, Luxulyan Bank, required the best expertise of both men on the footplate and a (hoped-for) similar response from the locomotive.

Perhaps the bank that presented most problems for the St Blazey crews was on the line to Fowey, where from Par the gradients were 1 in 50 with a short stretch of 1in 46 just before the 1,173 yard Pinnock tunnel. Heavy clay trains were worked by the hulking 42XX class 2-8-0Ts, normally confined to heavy coal trains in the South Wales valleys and St Blazey always had a couple for this work. Thanks to Michael Dyer, a former shunter at St Blazey yard I can record that that the loading for a unassisted 2-8-0T on a clay job was twenty 15 ton wagons; any more and a banker would be required from Par Bridge. For the crew on the train engine it would be a normal days work, slogging away up the incline, through the tunnel and out in to the fresh air to almost immediately come to a stop on the reverse slope of the eastern end of the tunnel, by Pinnock Tunnel Signal Box, alongside a STOP board, just in case you forgot. Such a 'stop board' commanded all goods trains to stop and await the arrival of the guard, a wretched figure who'd had to walk forward through a dark tunnel now choked with a dense yellow sulphurous smoke. Once at the head of the train he would pin down the brakes on the leading

wagons and more as the train moved slowly forward. As noted before, this made it easier to control the train on the 1 in 36 falling gradient towards Fowey. When the driver felt that sufficient brakes had been secured he would give two blasts on the whistle. The guard would then wait until his van came to him, jump aboard, and exchange a signal with the fireman to let him know that he was on board, for it was not unknown for a man to miss the grab handrail or otherwise slip, and fall. In dark or bad weather all the guard's signals had to be made waving a lamp, which didn't help! Once our guard was on the train he would set to with the big handbrake on the van, easing it a little at judicious moments. Probably worst off in all this were the two lost souls on the banking engine, which had come to rest perhaps mid-way in the tunnel, swirling with noxious fumes. The cab had immediately filled with the smoke from the train engine but of course the banker produced its own smoke too. Respite could not come until the train moved forward and they could follow on to the longed-for open air.

The smoke was so dense, legend has it, that the handrails on the banking engine would have a yellowish hue from the sulphur... Well, maybe – but it remains all too true that for the men on that engine, it was a desperate time. Gasping for some decent air to breathe, the only and fairly pitiful relief could come by lifting the square inspection plate set in the front

of the footplate, in an effort to draw up some relatively fresher air from the floor of the tunnel. This side of work on the footplate is seldom recorded. It was not always the sun and romance of holiday trains on the sea wall!

The April 1939 Great Western Railway *Appendix to the No.6 Section of the Service Timetable* makes mention of unusual feature of the tunnel. This was a 'clapper gong' fixed about twenty wagon lengths from the Fowey end and activated when a train went past. This gave an indication to the crew of the banker engine as to their position in the pitch-black tunnel. The banker engine, after the train had moved off without it, its services no longer needed, would then proceed to the Pinnock Tunnel Signal Box, and on instruction from the signalman ran back to Par Bridge.

Of interest also was the requirement for the banking engine to be coupled on the gradient from Par Bridge to the Tunnel, unlike on the South Devon banks where the assisting engine was uncoupled. So the uncoupling was done in blackness and swirling smoke. Trains seldom required banking engines on the eastern end of the line from Fowey towards Par because these were normally empty wagons and therefore not nearly as heavy as a loaded train.

Par Tunnel box closed on 27th January 1957; the track from Par Bridge to Fowey was lifted and the line closed in 1968. The track bed was then converted to a road

Left. A relic from the days of the Cornwall Railways, locomotive-outline weather vane and bell on the St Blazey works building, still there in September 1959. R.C. Riley, www.transporttreasury.co.uk

Above. At Par Docks a very low bridge under the Great Western main line required locomotives with unnaturally low clearance. This was the result, or one of them, built by Bagnall and named ALFRED, on 8 July 1955. A second locomotive had the name JUDY. ALFRED is still working on the Bodmin & Wenford Railway. R.C. Riley, www.transporttreasury.co.uk

Below. 6301, one of a couple of 2-6-0s usually to be found on the St Blazey complement. R.Parkes/C.Horsham.

Top. **The Coaster 'Simultineity' waits at Par docks for the dockside shunter to place clay wagons on the siding in order that the crane can start loading into her holds. R.C. Riley, www.transporttreasury.co.uk**

Middle. **Carne Point was once the principal deep-water port for the export of china clay and handled at one time 1.5 million tons/year. These are the jetties and sidings, with coasters being loaded from wagons tipping directly on to a shoot in the ship's hold, and a second by conveyor belt.**

Below. **No.4 Jetty on the Fowey River showing the impressive conveyor belt system for feeding the clay to vessels moored alongside the jetty.**

Top. No.4 Jetty from the river on 2 September 1954. R.C. Riley, www.transporttreasury.co.uk

Middle. East portal of the fearsome Pinnock Tunnel, 5 May 1957. 1,173 yards in length, it is situated at the summit of the 1 in 39 gradient on the St Blazey side of the line from Fowey to St Blazey. The rails have now been lifted and the tunnel and the trackbed is now paved as a road, and used by clay lorries. M. Dart.

Below. Liskeard on 10 July 1955; prairie tank 4508 has just departed from the branch platform on the way to Coombe Junction and Looe. Although on a falling gradient the train is restricted to a speed of 15mph. R.C. Riley, www.transporttreasury.co.uk

Top. Climbing up to Liskeard in the summer of 1948; the last leg of the journey from Coombe Junction – the 1 in 40 climb to the branch platform at Liskeard station.

Middle. An idyllic scene in the Looe Valley, on 10 July 1955. The 45XX and its train are leaving Coombe Junction (box in distance) for the ascent to Liskeard, after reversal. R.C. Riley, www.transporttreasury.co.uk

Below. On 18 July 1960 the Looe branch goods is 'framed' by the Moorswater Viaduct some 318 yards in length, at a height above the train of 147 feet. R.C. Riley, www.transporttreasury.co.uk

for English China Clay lorries, and the 1,173 yard tunnel was equipped with lighting for the first time in its history. No 'clapper gong' for the lorry drivers, who had it rather easy compared to the guard and banker crew, you couldn't help but observe, a bit ruefully perhaps.

At Fowey there were strict rules governing shunting operations, which involved pulling stock out on to the branch itself. The working had to conform with Train Staff Regulations though there might well have been a locally developed way round this, courtesy blind eyes all round. At night after the last train had cleared a 'staff' would be drawn from the apparatus at Fowey and retained in the box until the branch opened in the morning for the normal branch working. This in effect enabled shunting to go on with the branch classified as a siding.

The line from Burngullow and St Austell to Par required expert train handling due to the changes in severity of the falling gradient; there are sections as steep as 1 in 61 and 64 until reaching the lower parts. A fully laden clay train descending from Burngullow was required to stop after clearing the platform at St Austell to have brakes pinned down. This done, the train would proceed down the bank towards Par. The problem arose with the 'Par Hump'...

About one mile before Par the gradient suddenly changes from 1 in 61 falling to 1 in 100 rising for a short stretch before a fall again of 1 in 57 down to Par, a real roller-coaster. For most train crews it would be necessary to stop before the Par Hump, release the hand brakes on the wagons and proceed as per normal working practice. The problem was, this

was a busy main line and this method would almost invariably delay a following passenger train, with all the paper work which that could entail. As was often the case, the locals worked a way round this, contravening all Rules and Regulations of course, and as usual it was some way away from accepted 'good working'. Yet such unofficial procedures allowed the railway to keep working where otherwise it wouldn't and until or if anything untoward happened everyone was happy.

So it was that the St Blazey men had worked out their own way to avoid the stop at the Par Hump. Their trick was to let the train run (I've been told it was akin to running away) at sufficient, but low, speed on the approach to the Hump. This kept the couplings and buffers closed up so that weight alone carried the locomotive and train over the hump without faltering and without a slackening of the couplings. The problem was; misjudge it and you are over the top and falling again towards Par, only this time without any additional braking to help. Now all this is somewhat alarming; it left so much to chance that my first thoughts were that this was another leg-pull; after all, we were in a pub! But no, my big brother was perfectly serious and the antics really did happen. It all seemed pretty scary to me, but, if I may make a tribute as a former Laira footplateman to those St Blazey men, I am sure that we could not have done it better, if at all!

All clay wagons, it will be clear by now, were loose-coupled and thus individually unbraked; they could not be braked from the footplate. The couplings were three steel chain links, each some twelve inches

in length, so there was no way to tighten them up. Fully extended, a gap remained of a few inches between the buffers, and one of the most familiar sounds to anyone of a couple of generations back was the links 'clanking' as they tightened when a goods train started train to pull away from a stop, or the closing together of the buffers taking up the spaces as the brakes were applied. Working a train over an undulating stretch of track, such as we had in abundance in the West Country, as I've already said (more than once!) made demands of skill and experience from the driver and guard, as well as the fireman beyond most everyday tasks. It was imperative to avoid any undue 'snatching' of the couplings, causing a link to break, thereby dividing the train.

I've also touched before on the ingrained conviction at Laira, passed down through generations, that we and our work were at the top of the tree. As I've hinted at already, Newton Abbot might be the Division 'HQ' but this was clearly some organisational blunder, to be resolved one day, while the sheds to the west, in Cornwall, while not exactly country bumpkins, enjoyed only limited horizons of geography, intellect, etc. Laira, it seemed to us, was clearly not only the premier engine shed in the West of England, but indeed on the whole of the Great Western system, after only Old Oak Common and that only because everything in London had to be bigger than anywhere else. No other shed could match the quality of our work. It followed, inevitably therefore, that the experience and expertise of the Plymouth footplatemen, helped a little by their train guards, in handling any sort of train was

With the estuary on one side and the trees on the skyline we are not far from Terras Crossing.

Yes, here we are, standing on the crossing. No train, but a fine view of the Looe River Estuary. A pity the tide is out!

unsurpassable! Or so we all thought, and were brought up to believe. That is until one looked honestly at the work on the clay branches by St Blazey men – as we have indeed done.

Gradients were severe in many places and sprinkled throughout the working timetable were the words 'Stop Board', something we became familiar with during the operations at Pinnock tunnel. It required the train to be brought to a halt at the top of an incline to have handbrakes pinned down on the wagons to increase the braking. In some instances the falling gradient was not so severe and was followed by a reverse change of rising gradient. The driver would have the locomotive brake, the fireman the tender handbrake, and the guard in the van at the rear would be applying his brake too. Travelling down gradient would have all of the buffers on the wagons tightly compressed together as with their weight they strained to push forward and run with the gradient. The difficulty occurred at the bottom with the change in the gradient from falling to rising; the driver would have to open the regulator once again to tackle the up-grade. The skill was in that transition. The brakes had to be eased off so as to allow the wagons to gently move apart from each other and the slack in the couplings to take up. Get it wrong – too fierce, and the wagons would open up with a terrific snatch and in all probability this would be so powerful as to break a link in a coupling. Even if that did not happen the jolt at the back would probably throw

the guard off balance as he was working the handbrake on the van platform. Injuries were far from unknown. For us at Laira, work of this nature would come about possibly one week in four. For the St Blazey men it was a way of life!

****

I am not sure if Jim Perryman was on duty at the St Blazey coal stage on the occasion of this story or not, but he was very sure of the facts. One Jeff Kimber, a reprobate, had decided that the coal stage gang were fair game for one of the more outlandish practical jokes and, after some covert but probably not over-intelligent planning (these were not original; rather they were handed down the generations) he waited one night until the coal was getting low in the wagons and the work tailing off. The trap was sprung. Carrying a set of old overalls Jeff climbed the ladder up to the water tank and thrust them into the chimney, blocking it. At the same time Barry Sullivan was to jam the cabin door with a coal pick through the handles, situated conveniently on the outside. Thus no escape was possible. Donald Tabb and Bill Rundle had charge of the water hose normally used to damp down the hot coals and ash cleared out from fireboxes and smokeboxes. They trained the hose on the cabin door, ready. At a signal from Jeff who had climbed down from the water tank, and when the increasingly hysterical shouts, threats and curses from inside the cabin had indicated a sufficient level of distress in the smoke-filled mess room, Barry was signalled to release the

coal pick permitting the doors to be opened. As the coal men staggered out with streaming eyes and much coughing and spluttering, Donald and Bill turned the water on to play a jet of water at the doorway...

The perpetrators were by now disappearing in the direction of the toilet block; lately but children, their instinct was to hide in cubicles, a simple-mindedness in contrast to the complexities of the plot which almost guaranteed retribution. Donald wisely disappeared altogether while Jeff and Barry in one lavatory cubicle were able to force the door closed with their booted feet against the coal men's onslaught. A naïve Bill Rundle crouched in an adjoining cubicle giggled as Jeff and Barry were discovered. Failing to breach their particular citadel the enraged coal men's attention turned to the adjacent cubicle and it suddenly dawned on my luckless brother that his situation did not really warrant giggling. Not at all. In burst the coal stage men; the next few minutes of Bill's life were unpleasant, in the way that cuts and bruises are unpleasant. With this the coal men were content; Bill carried the can but that was the way of it. For the coal stage men honour had been satisfied. Jeff, Barry and Donald were happy for they had got away with it. Foreman Fred Bishop would certainly have caught wind of events (a gaffer relied on his intelligence network and in any event he'd have seen/done it all before) but that familiar old blind eye swung into action and no disciplinary procedures ever resulted.

Top. Nearing St Keyne, and the estuary not to be seen. The woodland is still worth a glance though.

Middle. Looe station in August 1948. Derek Clayton.

Below. A view from the platform looking towards the town and beach, in the summer of 1948. This area has now disappeared and is built upon.

Top. While his fireman takes on water for the Bodmin branch 2-6-2T, the driver waves to Truro's 2-6-0 6300 at the head of a down goods train. The leading clay wagons are destined for Par or Fowey and would have come either from Lee Mill or Moorswater clay 'dries'.

Middle. 14XX 0-4-2T 1419 waiting at Fowey with the 5.35pm to Lostwithiel on 31 May 1960. This was the last branch in Cornwall worked by an auto train. L.R. Freeman, www.transporttreasury.co.uk

Bottom. The Looe branch platform at Liskeard, 31 May 1960. L.R. Freeman, www.transporttreasury.co.uk

Top. Small prairie 4565 running round for a Looe train at Liskeard, 31 May 1960 L.R. Freeman, www.transporttreasury.co.uk

Middle. Looe, looking north on 31 May 1960. L.R. Freeman, www.transporttreasury.co.uk

Bottom. Moorswater shed, 31 May 1960. L.R. Freeman, www.transporttreasury.co.uk

Then there was the donkey... Somehow an innocent *Equus africanus asinus*, without the knowledge or consent of the owner it has to be presumed, was led – stolen – from wherever it was quietly grazing to land up in the engine shed. Anyone with a knowledge of the temperament of these beasts will know that this would have been no mean feat. The incentive, it was said, was a carrot waved invitingly across its nostrils but that seems to owe more to the cartoons than any reality. It must have had at least a string round its neck. One version of the tale has the animal discovered by chargehand Fred Bishop locked in the cleaners cabin amid copious droppings but the truth was probably something different. The poor beast was tethered to office door of timekeeper clerk Raymond Snell, with a cardboard sign swinging from its neck. BOOK US ON, RAY it read. The ripples of this incident made themselves felt for some time; the name of a mysterious fireman, 'N.Eddy' might appear on the roster sheet, or a fireman's skills unflatteringly compared to those of a donkey, who at least could have used two shovels. An as(s)inine story in every way.

Top. **Coombe Junction looking north to the Moorswater Viaduct, 31 May 1960. It was an idyllic setting; the path on the right led to cottages and the hamlet above the valley. L.R. Freeman, www.transporttreasury.co.uk**

Right. **Coombe Junction, looking south to Looe. The Junction signal box can just be seen in the distance, with the platforms of the halt on the left beyond the crossover, 31 May 1960. L.R. Freeman, www.transporttreasury.co.uk**

The yard at Looe with customary small prairie, in this case 5570, running round a train on 31 May 1960. The signalman stands ready with the carrier of the single line 'tablet', to give to the fireman for the return to Coombe Junction. L.R. Freeman, www.transporttreasury.co.uk

Left. 5570 running round earlier on during the journey of the 1.23pm Liskeard-Looe at Coombe Junction, 31 May 1960. L.R. Freeman, www.transporttreasury.co.uk

Below. 5557 at Par with the 10.40am ex-Newquay, 31 May 1960. Note the ever-present 'pep' pipe dangling from the cab. This will be used repeatedly during bunker first running. It was effectively a hosepipe and, played against the coal, would keep dust to a minimum. L.R. Freeman, www.transporttreasury.co.uk

Top. 2-6-2T 5557 with the 10.40am to Par, at Newquay on 31 May 1960. Surprisingly for a bank holiday the platform and carriages seem deserted. Everyone must be at the beach! L.R. Freeman, www.transporttreasury.co.uk

Middle. 5557 at Liskeard with train from Looe, 17 August 1958. Summer traffic on the branch was heavy; the passengers are walking to the main line platforms, running at right angles behind the photographer. A.E. Bennett, www.transporttreasury.co.uk

Bottom. 5557 at Looe with train for Liskeard 17 August 1958. Note the unusual water tower/tank, not a GW product at all and surely a relic from Liskeard, Caradon and Looe Railway days. A.E. Bennett, www.transporttreasury.co.uk

5557 after arrival at Looe 17 August 1958. It will draw ahead to then run round the train for the journey back. A.E. Bennett, www.transporttreasury.co.uk

St Blazey pannier tank 7715 in the sidings at Fowey; a train is signalled for the through road.

It is said of Cornishmen that they are often 'silent thinkers'! If this be true then surely Fireman Rex Pope (left) and Driver Dennis Beer (right) of St Blazey shed conform to type as they regard the photographer from the cab of 5531. Terry Nicholls.

Melangoose Mill Works; the settling tanks are at the rear of the coal fired kilns - known as 'linhays'. When settled, and the clay has dried, it would be cut into blocks for shipment either by rail or water. The branch line continues to Meledor Mill, bottom right.

Chapter 6
St Blazey Branch Line Working

Ponts Mill Branch

As far back as records show, Ponts Mill was the highest navigational point on the Par river, and it was there that a china stone mill and pan kilns were established. Certain of the areas of clay workings had not been subject to the same degree of geological change as that of the clay pits, and the residue had stayed as a stone rather than the finer mica (clay). So it was known as 'china stone'. In many cases these china stone quarries were alongside the clay pits. The working of the stone involved crushing it to a fine powder, a product much prized by the manufacturers of high-grade porcelain. Hence the 'mills' were in fact stone crushing mills.

Served first by canal and then a horse-worked tramway, the Cornwall Minerals Railway undertook the improvement of the existing Treffry Railway, creating a new line from Par Docks through St Blazey and Ponts Mill to Luxulyan. Avoiding the Carmears incline and the aqueduct, the new route effectively cut off the Ponts Mill works. To remedy this a siding was constructed to join with the new line at St Blazey Bridge. In the 1950s the place was still served by a train which left St Blazey yard at 8.30am for the three quarter mile journey to the mill. Once there the locomotive, a pannier tank most likely, did any shunting that might be necessary and returned with the loaded wagons about 10am, leaving the empties it had brought for the next day. The nature of the sidings was such that the April 1939 *Appendix* to the Working Timetable permitted, unusually I'd have to say, the 'propelling' of wagons from St Blazey yard to Ponts Mill, providing that the number of wagons did not exceed 30, and that a brake van should be the leading vehicle. Speed was restricted to eight miles an hour, and both guard and shunter were required to ride in the van. This seemed a little redundant, for the former would be there anyway and the latter would plump for the comfort of the van and a seat rather than the crowded footplate, though the journey was of course one of only minutes.

The signalman at St Blazey Bridge box had to extract an electric train token for the section from his box to Luxulyan, which had keys to lock and unlock all the necessary points. The token was issued to the guard or shunter, 'leading' in the van and after setting the points for the siding to Ponts Mill, one of them would ensure that the train had passed through and cleared the junction. After that the 'main' line was reset by inserting the token in the token box, turning it to secure it, and telephoning the signalman to this effect. This effectively permitted the safe use of the through line once more. The same procedure was carried out on the return journey, only this time in the reverse order, and upon completion the token was delivered back to the signalman and replaced in the original apparatus. The mill ceased to operate in 1965 and the line sadly closed. It had been worked latterly by a diesel shunter.

Goonbarrow Junction-Carbean Sidings

This 3½ mile line was constructed to serve the china clay kilns around Bugle, Stenalees and Carthew, diverging from the Newquay line approximately half a mile below Bugle station. The line circled around the village of Bugle and ran through typical china clay countryside with the conical waste heaps and numerous clay 'dries' and associated buildings. On rising gradients for most of it's length of 1 in 32 to 1 in 65, the only more or less level track was at Rosevear at the beginning of the branch and from Gunheath to Carbean at the furthest point. At approximately half way the line passed through the 341 yard long Stenalees tunnel, on a rising gradient of 1 in 39.

In 1951 the Goonbarrow branch was served by two trains a day. The first left St Blazey yard at 7.50 am, with some fifteen or so empty wagons and called 'as required' at the sidings at Rosevear, Wheal Henry, Old Beam, Imperial, the two Caudledown sidings and Gunheath to eventually arrive at the end of the line at Carbean Siding. The locomotives by this time were the little 16XX pannier tanks, favoured because of the shorter wheelbase, which reduced the wear on the flanges of the wheels due to the extreme curvature of the track. This train returned from Carbean at 11.30am, collecting laden wagons on the way, and required all the skill of the train crew in negotiating the falling gradient, for this was a heavy train for such a small locomotive. The guard was called to assist with the pinning down of brakes between Gunheath and Caudledown where one of our famous 'Stop Boards' stood sentinel at the top of the severest section, to Wheal Henry. The train was booked to arrive back at St Blazey yard at 1.30 pm. A second, similar train (such was the clay

Carlyon Farm Kiln on the Trenance clay branch – as a young lad I always knew the line as 'Bojea'. The line extended northwards up the valley for almost two miles to reach the clay workings at Lansalson.

0-6-0PT 3705 shunting the sidings at Carlyon Farm. Ahead of the locomotive the Bojea siding is on the left and the line to Lansalson to the right.

output back then) left St Blazey at 12.30 pm, arriving Carbean at 3.0 pm. Leaving again after half an hour, it arrived back at St Blazey at 5.20 pm.

Carbis Branch
The Carbis branch, only 1 mile 50 chains in length, left the Newquay line via Bugle goods yard and ran alongside the Newquay line for a short distance before changing direction westwards where the gradient began to increase to the steepest section at Wheal Prosper of 1 in 44. In addition to the pit, Wheal Prosper consisted of a kiln and brickworks, and because the complex was situated alongside the road to a small hamlet called Carbis, it became known as Carbis Wharf. A feature of Wheal Prosper was the giant square chimney which dominated the surrounding area.

The 'Wheal Rose branch' was a short spur extended beyond the Carbis line, again west, to serve the Wheal Rose Clay Works. The clay trains were worked by St Blazey locos, normally 16XX pannier tanks after their introduction about 1950.

Retrew/Meledor Mill Branch
St Dennis Junction was not only the northern extent of the line from Burngullow but was also the connection for the Retrew Mill branch, opened in 1874 to Melangoose Mill, extended to Retrew and Meledor Mill in 1912, whereupon it was re-named the Retrew/ Meledor Mill branch. The branch was notable in that it enjoyed a falling gradient for its entire length. The steepest section, 1 in 41, was at Virginia Crossing, approximately half-way between Retrew Crossing and what we called 'the loop' (to enable the loco to run round) and Meledor Mill. Virginia Crossing had special working instructions as there was no run-round loop. Empty clay wagons for loading at Meledor Mill and Virginia

Siding were firstly allowed to 'gravitate' there into the siding at Melangoose Mill under the control of the guard or travelling shunter using the handbrakes on the wagons. The train would then reverse back until the locomotive could gain access to the sidings, drop in to collect the wagons, attach them to the front of the engine, bring them out of the siding and propel them forward into the sidings at Virginia and Meledor.

Traffic was heavy and St Blazey usually put 45XX small prairie 2-6-2Ts on the job. The Newquay branch had a through connection to Burngullow and thus to St Blazey and Par; not all trains from St Dennis Junction returned to St Blazey via the Newquay branch itself but were scheduled to make their way to the main line at Burngullow, instead.

Gothers Tramway
This was a 3ft gauge tramway, built in 1879, which extended south-east from St Dennis Junction to Domelick Siding and the Gothers clay works. Even as clay pits were being closed, Gothers was to play a part in an experimental programme to find a use for the millions of tons of sand which were being accumulated. A plant was established to grade the sand for various industrial purposes including building. A pilot scheme operated by a local firm, Selleck Nicholls & Co. Ltd., to use the waste sand to make pre-cast concrete panels, led to the construction of what were to be called 'Cornish Unit Houses'. The fine grade of sand from Gothers was perfect for the purpose apparently. From these beginnings the industry has expanded, establishing further plants producing all manner of building materials, from specialised calcium silicate bricks to the common concrete block. The original clay works and tramway fell by the wayside early on, closing in 1942.

Trenance Valley Branch
The branch enjoyed differing names. It is 'Trenance Valley' in the GWR 1939 working timetable, yet the succeeding 1951 timetable has instead 'St Austell, Trenance Junction and Lansalson'. To those born and bred in the area, among which I count myself, and to the railwaymen of St Austell and St Blazey it was always just 'Bojea'. Just 1 mile 39 chains in length, the branch diverged from the main line on the up side just west of St Austell station, before the Trenance viaduct. Completed in 1920, it served firstly the Carroncarrow Kiln and the Trenance sidings adjacent to the main line, the clay works at Carlyon Farm Sidings, Bojea Sidings, Lower Ruddle and Boskell Sidings and Lansalson.

With ruling gradients of 1 in 40/43 as the branch climbed its way up to Hensbarrow, instructions were issued for the securing of wagons during shunting operations, to protect the 'main' line from runaway wagons. It was known for the shunting operations at times to be a little haphazard and wagons once brought to a standstill might not always have the handbrake properly pinned down. With the vibration of the locomotive going by (on the loop line) or for no obvious reason, a wagon would suddenly just start to move!

There was also a strict speed restriction of 10 mph. The branch had just one mineral train a day in 1951, booked to leave St Austell at 8.10am and arrive at Lansalson at 8.33am. After shunting the train departed at 9.15am for St Austell, arriving at 9.44am. A further freight, rather than mineral train was booked on the branch, leaving St Austell at 2.15 pm for Trenance Valley sidings. It arrived a little over ten minutes later at 2.28, returning at 2.43 and arriving back at St Austell at 2.56 pm. St Blazey customarily provided one of its 45XX 2-6-2Ts for the

'Bojea' branch jobs. Trenance Valley itself had four sidings, labelled conventionally Nos.1, 2, 3 and 4; the latter three could hold 25 wagons while No.1 was always kept clear for the locomotive to run round the train. Lower Ruddle's Siding lay on the steepest section of the line, and the usual instructions were issued for the pinning down of brakes on the wagons in the sidings, to prevent any unwanted movement resulting in the blockage of the running line.

Personally, this little branch always seemed a bit 'special' to me. The reason had little to do with the clay industry, but instead a somewhat tenuous family link, nonetheless important to me. As the line began to work its way north it entered Trenance Wood past, on the right, Menacuddle Farm; the adjacent Menacuddle House was the home of the Hicks family who also founded and owned THE St Austell Brewery, situated below the farm in Trevanion Road. Prior to September 1939, when my Territorial Army father was called up for war service, he had been a gardener at Menacuddle, and worked for George Hicks.

Burngullow to St Dennis Junction
The line was originally called the Newquay and Cornwall Junction Railway, and connected the Cornwall Railway main line with the Par-Newquay line at St Dennis. It opened from Burngullow to Drinnick Mill, just south of Nanpean, in 1869. Financial difficulties meant that it was not until 1874 that connection was made to St Dennis Junction, increasing the length

of the line to seven miles. Here again steep gradients of 1 in 40/44 and very sharp curves, some with a radius as tight as 18 chains, required short wheelbase locos and once again the little 16XX pannier tanks succeeded to the work in the 1950s, though the stronger 57XXs were used too, especially when loads were at their heaviest. Sometimes the clay trains were double headed with a pair of pannier tanks. The gradient up from Par to St Austell is severe, as much as 1 in 61 in places and I am told that the sight and sound of two pannier tanks with a full load of empty clay wagons between them was something to tell the grandchildren about. I would liked to have seen and heard them.

A sample working of interest is the 12.55 pm St Blazey to Drinnick Mill, which had a 57XX 0-6-0PT as train engine but was assisted by a second 57XX coupled up in front for the climb from Par to St Austell. Once there it came off from the train and thereafter worked as the yard pilot. The bank was 1 in 94 and I often wonder what a sight it must have been.

I have briefly mentioned the Burngullow to Drinnick Mill and St Dennis Junction mineral line in Chapter Five and, similarly, the Par to St Dennis Junction and Newquay in an earlier chapter. In as much as the workings of the clay traffic were concerned, they were used for a 'through service' by one train each day working from St Blazey yard. The first train of the day was the 'through' service and left St Blazey yard at 5.35am for Drinnick Mill, running via St Dennis

Junction. It left the Junction at 6.45am on a rising gradient, calling as required at Whitegate; Parkandillick and Great Treviscoe Sidings. The next sidings were at Kernick which was equipped with a Ground Frame and also was a crossing point, on the only level section of track. Again calling 'as required', came the sidings at Little Treviscoe, Goonvean, Slip, Luke's New and Luke's Old Sidings, to the West of England Sidings which was effectively the 'top of the bank' where the gradient changed to falling to the first destination at Drinnick Mill. Providing the intermediate working was not to excess, the train was due to reach here at 7.30am.

Shunting at Drinnick Mill took place until the departure time at 9.40am with the destination now Burngulow, west of St Austell on the Penzance main line. Surprisingly this train was not required to call at any of the works on the way and other than stopping to put down brakes for assistance at the exotically named Drubbers No.1 Siding and again after High Street on the falling gradients, was due at Burngullow at 10.10am. A second train ran from St Blazey via St Dennis, destination Drinnick Mill, with a similar working pattern as the earlier train and arriving at 10.50am. The return working departed at 12 noon, this time returning to St Dennis Junction, calling as required at all the sidings to collect the loaded wagons of clay. Falling gradients on this stretch required the pinning down of brakes at Luke's Old Siding, Luke's New Siding and at Parkandillick. Arrival at the Junction was just after 1pm. The

The China Clay industry was noted for being labour intensive. Very little machinery was in use and 'elbow grease ' was the order of the day. The dried clay had to be manhandled firstly into wheelbarrows and then loaded into railway wagons. It was said that eight fills of a clayman's shovel made 1cwt – 160 shovelfuls to the ton. A railway wagon might hold several tons, a lot of shovelfuls! And they did this day in day out with just a break for 'croust' (Cornish for 'crib' or any meal break). A pasty perhaps and a swig of something from a bottle!

Above. St Dennis Junction in July 1955. Pannier tank 3675 leaves with a clay train for St Blazey with banking assistance for the first part of the journey from 'small prairie' 4526. To the right of the signal box are the lines to Meledor Mill, (where the clay had probably originated) and to Drinnick Mill and Burngullow. R.C. Riley, trans porttreasury.co.uk

Middle. The driver of St Blazey 2-8-0T 4294 is replenishing the oil cups on the 'slide bars', the parts the 'cross head' of the pistons glided through on every stroke. The fireman will also be busy, trimming the bunker and tidying up the footplate. With certain route restrictions it is probable that the 42XX has brought a train of empties up from St Blazey, and is waiting for the smaller locomotives to bring loaded wagons from the branches for the return journey. St Blazey always had two of this class on shed for the heavy clay workings. Keith Bachelor.

Bottom. Pannier tank 3733, the engine involved in the fatal accident at Burngullow on 9th June 1952. I have recounted this story elsewhere in the book. The angle of the bunker gives an idea of the force of the clay wagons which piled on the back of the locomotive at the time of impact. Keith Batchelor.

first of two short distance trains destined for New Carpellsa Sidings departed from Burngullow at 10.30am (8.45am Sats) but was only booked to call 'as required' at High Street Sidings. Arrival at Carpella was 10.45 (9am on Sats). Departure was at 1.20am (9.30am Sats) with an arrival at Burngullow of 11.50am (9.45am Sats). The last train of the day departed from Burngullow at 2pm for Drinnick Mill arriving at 2.45pm, departing again at 4.10pm arriving at Burngullow at 4.35pm.

****

All did not always pass without incident and perhaps the most fateful took place on Monday 9th June 1952. St Blazey driver Percival Short and his fireman Jack Hooper were on a return working with a

Top. Four St. Blazey men sit in the front of the second locomotive in the Burngullow incident, 2-6-2T 4545. Buffer beam bent back and the two bracing struts buckled up like pieces of wire. I feel sure that the thoughts of these men would have been with the family of Driver Short. Keith Batchelor.

Middle. Journeys end for these horses having hauled their heavy clay wagon along the country lanes and main road from the Clay Dries at Burngullow to the St Austell terminus of the Pentewan railway. From here the clay will be loaded on to the wagons of the narrow gauge railway to be transported down the valley to the dockside at Pentewan Harbour.

Left. In addition to clay being transported 'loose' in open wagons, it was also carried in 2 cwt wooden casks. In every district of the claylands there would also be a cooperage. The casks (barrels) would be collected by horse and wagon and taken to the particular 'dry' or 'linhay' as some were known. It looks that about 20 of these casks have made a load for this horse, which if they were full would be much too heavy.

train of twenty full clay wagons from Drinnick Mill. Driver Short brought his engine, 57XX pannier 3733 and train to a halt at the stop board at the top of the bank above New Carpella sidings for the guard, Jack Ede, to pin down the required number of brakes on the leading wagons. When he was satisfied with the additional braking, and his guard safely back in the van, driver Short steadily eased the heavy train down the gradient. With expertise born of long years on the job he worked at the engine brake while his fireman assisted on the handbrake. All seemed to be going well. Suddenly before Lanjeth, and apparently without good reason, the weight of the train seemed to be too much for 3733 and the braking, and the train gradually took control. Approaching Lanjeth it was estimated by startled onlookers to be travelling at speeds around 60 mph. With driver Short desperately trying to regain control, the train crashed through the level crossing gates.

Every effort came to nought and there were no more options open to the crew; the train was running away out of control and their fate was in the balance. Driver Short ordered the fireman to jump for his life and Jack Hooper did just that, and other than a few scratches was by great good fortune unharmed. Guard Ede saw the fireman abandoning the footplate and promptly followed suit, saving his own life thereby, in all probability. Percival Short, though his fireman had begged him to jump too, nonetheless remained on his engine, still desperate to find a way of stopping his train. Blowing the whistle again, a 'clone' as we termed it, to inform all and sundry that his train was running away, he continued his efforts all the way to Burngullow. This was to cost him his

life. At Burngullow the line was blocked by 2-6-2T 4545, shunting across the line. Pannier tank 3733 with Percival on the footplate ploughed into the other locomotive with disastrous results. Percival Short was eventually pulled from beneath the wreckage and taken to the Royal Cornwall Hospital at Truro. His injuries were so severe that he later died. When the gradient charts for the majority of these clay lines are examined it is surprising that more accidents of this sort did not occur.

I hope the reader will not mind if we wander off that which is strictly 'railway'; on the St. Blazey workings, I briefly mentioned horse-drawn wagons at the beginning of the chapter, for instance.

They were known as 'drays' locally, and were very much a part of life in my boyhood. Before the general advent of motor transport the steam lorry was about the most advanced form of road vehicle but all the clay for the docks back then went in ancient and original fashion, in horse-drawn wagons. At East Hill in the south of St Austell for instance, clay was taken by horse cart to what was called the 'depot', where clay was loaded into wagons on a 2ft 6in narrow gauge mineral line for transport to Pentewan Harbour and export. The port of Charlestown, as already noted, had no rail connection and was entirely dependent upon the horse drawn convoys of carts, until lorries took over.

Full casks loaded on to a larger wagon at the 'linhay' for despatch to the nearest railway siding. The load looks to be 75 to 80 casks and at two cwts a prodigious one for the horses. The waggoner seems unconcerned at least as he leans against the shafts contemplating the journey ahead.

After arrival at the sidings it is again manual labour to get the casks in the railway wagons. By the number of casks stacked on the platform it looks a though these men have plenty of work 'in hand'!

Most of the clay taken to these places came from the clay 'dries' in the Burngullow area, and lumbered along Burngullow Lane, past Poltarrow Farm, now a holiday camp, down the steep narrow lane to Coyte, where my boyhood was spent, and then up the steep incline to St Mewan school to join the main Truro to St Austell road. I say 'lumbered', because the wagons were sturdily built and carried about four tons of dried clay cut in blocks approximately the size of a loaf of bread.

The carts were of an ancient sort which must have existed unchanged in Europe for a thousand years or more; I can imagine salt carts labouring over the steppes in like fashion in the days of the Visigoths. Each wagon had four heavy iron-bound wooden wheels, which ate large potholes in the unmetalled roads over which they passed. The horses often numbered three; a main horse fully harnessed and a second horse, with a complex arrangement of pulling chains and so on. A third horse, wearing harness similar to the second, was either led or tied to the back of the wagon and was brought into use for the inclines, of which there was no shortage. When the waggoner came to a steep downhill section the third horse would be attached by the 'pulling chains', to the rear of the wagon, with the intention of 'holding back', and acting as a brake.

Of course, as with everywhere in Cornwall, a section of downhill leads to a section of uphill and then the third horse would be attached to the leading horse so that there were three in front of the wagon. That was quite a sight to see and these wagons would be using the roads all day and every day for weeks on end. An added feature on the wagon was the 'drug', a metal shoe placed under one of the rear wheels of the wagon to act as a 'skid', stopping the wheel and therefore aiding the braking. It was this as much as the heavy loads on the wheels which damaged the surface of the road.

No matter how many horses were used it seemed the waggoners knew them all by name, and could be heard praising them, berating them, and generally chatting to them. They were a magnificent sight as they strained against their collars, leaning almost horizontal as they reached the steepest sections. The top of the climb from St Mewan School was known as Rocky Park. It was the site for the visiting circus, and the then home of St Austell Speedway Club; the horses would surely have welcomed it for it was also the start of the long down section that would last almost for the rest of the journey.

At times a waggoner on a Par run would take short cut through Fore Street, the main street in St Austell. It was narrow, and there was nearly always traffic chaos. China clay is an awkward material and so fine that it 'gets everywhere'; it 'sticks everywhere' too! There were always problems for the locals; the carts for instance would be piled high with blocks of clay, and inevitably every so often one or more would be dislodged and fall to the road. There they were crushed by the following wagons and when it rained a white quagmire formed; when the sun shone there were dust storms instead! Yet no one was heard to complain because after all, it was a part of our way of life; indeed we were dependent on it just as colliers were dependent on coal; it put food on the table. I wonder if the present generation would see it the same way.

Most of this is history of course and though the clay is still often obvious in the landscape, other than that which still goes by rail, the clay is either piped as slurry direct to the docks, or goes by lorry. It was a fact that even as locomotives needed sustenance in the form of coal and water to keep them going, so did the horses; the analogy was recognised right from the first, when the earliest sheds were called engine stables; locos when parked out of use awaiting the next job are still 'stabled' to this day. Dobbin's needs were more modest of course, a feed of oats from a bag hung from the collar, a couple of times a day, and a bucket of water, and they would go all day, and not a complaint.

One of the new Warship diesels, D816 ECLIPSE, incongruously hauling a train of four wheeled covered clay wagons at St Blazey yard, 20 July 1960. The semi-roundhouse engine shed is in the left background. R.C. Riley, www.transporttreasury.co.uk

The Truro River and the Quay (left) where the Radio Cornwall studios are now located. The Cathedral with its three spires rises above all. Reflections can be seen in the water. Courtesy Peter Manning.

Boscawen Street, Truro. A view looking from Victoria Square, probably in the 1920s, from the look of things. A notable feature of the street is that the paving setts are of Cornish granite. The imposing building at the end, central, was originally the Coinage Hall; it became a branch of Lloyds Bank which moved yet again to the imposing building on the right.

Chapter 7
Truro Engine Shed

Truro shed had passenger and goods workings for the 4-6-0s and the 2-6-0 and in latter years at least had a share in a through working to Newton Abbot and back with the 10.35 am London train. The Chacewater-Newquay line made possibly the greatest demand on the 45XX 2-6-2Ts, the largest engines permitted to work the line. Occasionally a 57XX pannier tank would be seen, but this was the exception; the branch was very much the domain of the '45s' and '55s'. A variety of locomotives could be found on the Falmouth branch, while both prairies and panniers could be seen on the goods line to Newham.   I can list some of the staff for the period about 1956; the Shed Master had been Joe Stevens, who was liked and respected by both drivers and fireman. He was appointed to Truro having previously served at Penzance. Joe was easily recognised as he walked around his domain, from his trademark black Homburg hat.

Frank Taylor, big in every sense of the word, succeeded to the position about 1956. He was unmatched in the multifarious skills and arts of running an engine shed, and at Truro he earned to respect of all those in his charge. Sadly Frank died suddenly just before the end of he steam age and although much saddened by his death, most of the staff at Truro agreed that Frank would have had it no other way, before his beloved

steam locomotives were withdrawn and scrapped. He was replaced by Jim Stone until the closure in 1962. Other figures were:

Foremen Edwin Oakes, Arthur Soper
Relief Foreman (Senior Driver) John Bearde
Chargehand Cleaner Cliff Webb.

The workings were covered by three links:

No.1 (Senior Link) covered the main line Penzance to Plymouth (Tavistock Junction).

Nos.2 and 3 covered the three branches; Chacewater to Tolcarn Junction on the Par Newquay Line, Truro to Falmouth and to Newham alongside the Truro River, detailed as below.

I am grateful to Ken and Muriel Vigus, railwayman and railwaywoman, for this information. Ken started his career in 1952 as a lad porter at Chacewater station, progressing to full porter and then shunter. He eventually trained to be a signalman and was stationed at Truro. Muriel was born into a railway family. She followed in the tradition in 1955 and became a booking clerk at Truro station. Muriel's father was Jack Thomas, an examiner at the extensive carriage and wagon workshops which adjoined the north side of the engine shed. The foreman here was George Coleman. Along with Muriel's father there were two other wagon examiners, Cyril Pascoe and Bill Day. The carriage and wagon shops

were destined to close in 1962 at the same time as the engine shed. The site is now is occupied by an agricultural merchant.

Chacewater to Tolcarn Junction and Newquay, 18miles 49chains

The original junction was triangular with approach roads from both east and west of Chacewater platform, thus permitting trains from the Newquay branch to be scheduled for either Penzance or Truro. The junction was originally controlled by no less than three signalboxes. In 1924 as an economy measure, the signal boxes were closed as was the west approach road, thus shutting off any direct service from the branch line to Penzance. A new single line independent of the main line to serve the branch was constructed from the northern face of Chacewater's island platform, running westwards for half a mile to Blackwater Junction, where it deviated on a long curve northwards towards Perranporth and Tolcarn Junction.

The line to Tolcarn Junction was built in two stages; first in 1903 to Perranporth, some seven miles and then in 1905 to Tolcarn Junction and thus to Newquay. The line was much welcomed, the Newquay shopkeepers it is said declaring a holiday and closing their shops, which seems an odd reaction to otherwise unlooked for crowds! It is reported that the Great Western decided against an official opening ceremony, providing a train outing instead for the Newquay and

Truro engine shed, April 1960. A view from the overbridge at the west end of the station platforms. It was a compact shed, set in the corner of ground below Highertown; engines were dealt with on those three nearest roads while the rest of the shed was for repairs or carriage and wagon work. Three 45XX 2-6-2Ts and two Hall 4-6-0s are visible in the running shed yard. The shed closed to steam in March 1962. R.C. Riley, www.transporttreasury.co.uk

To the left and a little beyond the coal stage was the turntable. Pannier tank 3709 sits comfortably whilst being turned. Her chimney is inexplicably missing the outer casing, which of course, 'set the whole thing off'. C. Howson.

Perranporth schoolchildren. The line officially closed in February 1963.

Intermediate stations and halts from Chacewater were: Mount Hawke, St Agnes, Goonbell, Mithian, Beach Halt (Perranporth), Perranporth; Goonhavern, Shepherds, Mitchell, Trewerry. The junction at Tolcarn was after Trewerry.

Truro to Falmouth 11 miles 67 chains

The branch left the main line to Penzance west of Truro at Penwithers Junction. It was built by the Cornwall Railway and opened in 1863, a considerable engineering effort with eight viaducts, three of them later converted to embankments, two tunnels and a couple of cuttings. After a steep climb away from Truro station, through Highertown tunnel, the branch continued from Penwithers Junction on a rising gradient of 1 in 66 for a mile to Penwithers cutting. After this came the first tunnel, at Sparnick, 490 yards long and cut through hard slate and shale. The gradient changes to 1 in 88 falling prior to the tunnel and steepens to 1 in 64 just before Perranwell station. From Perranwell the line is once more rising, at 1 in 66 but it eases as it reaches the second tunnel at Perran, 400 yards long. Perran like Sparnick was cut through slate and shale but it was not so strongly consolidated and a brick lining was provided throughout its length. From the tunnel the line changes direction and climbs again, at 1 in 60 for a mile or so to Ponsanooth viaduct and in to the very deep cutting at Roskrow Hill. From here the line falls at an average 1 in 60 gradient to Penryn. Falling again at 1 in 51 from Penryn to Collegewood viaduct there is then a slight rise on an embankment to Penmere platform, provided for the extra passengers as Falmouth developed westwards. From Penmere the line again falls, on a 1 in 80 gradient towards the station at Falmouth. Locomotives were predominantly the 45XX prairies and 57XX panniers but on a summer Saturday anything might appear, even a Castle with a through London train.

Truro to Newham Wharf 3 miles 33 chains

The Newham Wharf line left the Falmouth branch about a mile west of Truro station, at Penwithers, turning east and dropping down to the quays alongside the Truro River. There was a general speed restriction of 15mph and after leaving Penwithers the train was required to halt at the stop board at the head of a 1 in 52 falling gradient. Locomotives were the usual small prairies, the traffic consisting of coal for the gas works as well as feedstock and fertiliser.

There were normally two trains a day, except for Saturdays when only one ran; on Sundays of course nothing moved. The first train on a weekday left Truro yard at 6.50 am arriving at Newham 7.12; return was booked for 8.00 with an arrival time at Truro of 8.22. The second train left Truro at 5.08 pm leaving again after shunting at 6.25 to arrive back in Truro yard at 6.45 pm. The branch closed completely in November 1971.

Truro Goods Yard

For its size, Truro goods yard was very busy most of the time; not only with the marshalling of local traffic but with through goods trains setting down and picking up.****

I was pleased to meet and talk with Courtney Berryman, once a fireman at Truro shed. Courtney had started in the usual way as cleaner there in April 1956, and remained until 1968. He is now retired and a driver on the Bodmin and Wenford preserved railway line. As a cleaner boy Courtney remembers his first task was helping to clean 4099 KILGERRAN CASTLE, a Penzance locomotive which was to stand 'spare' for a Royal Train duty, in the unlikely event that the train engine

Passenger Schedules 1957

Chacewater dep.	Newquay arr.	Originated from
06.16	07.11	06.05 from Truro
07.25	08.32	07.13 from Truro
09.18	10.14	
10.24	10.43 Perranporth	10.10 from Truro
11.54	12.52	11.05 from Falmouth
13.35	14.34	
14.59	15.55	
15.57	16.20 Perranporth	08.25 from Paddington
16.39	17.36	16.25 from Truro
18.26	19.29	18.15 from Truro
20.00	20.55	19.10 from Falmouth
21.21	21.45 Perranporth	21.10 from Truro

Newquay dep.	Chacewater arr.	Destination
07.20	08.17	Redruth
07.35 Empty Stock	08.00	Perranporth
08.15 Perranporth	08.37	Paddington
09.12	10.07	Truro
11.00 Perranporth	11.21	Truro
11.50	12.47	
13.35	14.31	Truro
14.55	15.52	Truro
16.30 Perranporth	16.55	Truro
16.36	17.32	Truro
17.52	18.52	Truro
19.55	20.53	Truro
21.15	22.09	Truro

Passenger Schedules 1957

Truro dep.	Falmouth arr.	Originated from
05.35	06.04	Local(Truro)
06.53 Mixed Train	07.24	Local "
07.47	08.20	Local
08.26	08.57	Local
09.10	09.40	Local
10.15	10.46	Local
11.12	11.45	Local
11.37	12.09	Local
12.47	13.17	Local
13.40	14.11	Local
14.17	14.57	Local
14.57	15.30	Local
15.20	15.50	Local
15.49	16.18	Local
16.59	17.31	10.35 from Paddington
18.10	18.47	Local (Truro)
18 36	19.07	Local
19.35	20.06	13.45 from Bristol
20.11	20.40	Local
21.08	21.37	Local
21.55	22.23	Local

Falmouth dep.	Truro arr.	Destination
06.27	06.57	To Plymouth
08.00	08.29	Local (Falmouth)
08.35	09.07	To Paddington.
10.00	10.36	Local(Falmouth)
10.25	10.58	Local
11.00	11.35	To Newquay
11.25	12.00	Local(Falmouth)
12.10	12.40	Local
12.35	13.07	Local
13.30	14.02	Local
14.25	14.56	Local
15.10	15.40	Local
16.26	16.58	Local
17.10	17.41	Local
18.25	18.58	Local
19.10	19.38	Local
19.45	20.14	Local
20.55	21.28	Local
22.00	22.33	Local

got in trouble. Soon he was made fireman at Truro, for by this time the practice of making cleaners take the first available fireman vacancy, wherever it was, was breaking down as the shadows lengthened for steam. Indeed the first main line diesels worked into Cornwall as early as 1958.

He was first teamed up with driver Bruce Hewings to work the first goods of the day, the 2.0 am Truro-Newton Abbot. A coincidence struck me here, for when cycling in the early hours from Saltash to Laira, if the weather was wet, I used to cadge a lift on an early morning goods from Cornwall, if one was handy. On more than one occasion it was the 2.0 am from Truro. Anyway, booking on at 1.30 am, with the engine already prepared, they went off shed to collect the train in the Truro yard. This was always more or less a full load of 50 wagons or so, few if any of them vacuum braked. Truro men took the train as far as Tavistock Junction, arriving at about 5.30 am. The procedure then was to run all the way back west light engine to Plymouth North Road turntable, set in the triangle connecting the Millbay and Cornish Road with the station.

There they would turn and service the loco; oil, water, as necessary and then work back from Plymouth with the parcels that had left Paddington the night before. It was a hotchpotch of a train with parcels vans, fish vans, and even vans which had come from Liverpool overnight. The working normally had a Hall 4-6-0, though Courtney recalls that one week they had 6814 ENBOURNE GRANGE, often preferred in the hilly West to a Hall. It was in absolutely superb condition, beyond any normal running 'nick', even after overhaul at Swindon. The shed foreman revealed that ENBOURNE GRANGE had indeed been recently overhauled but had been taken out of the normal run of service and the entire cleaning gang set to work on it as if their very lives depended on it, for it had been selected for a Royal working.

In any talk between railwaymen of the glory days, the 'characters', both heroes and villains, soon come up, and so it was with Courtney and me. Of those firmly in the former category, St Blazey had driver Percy Kimber while I mentioned two at Laira, Edgar Stephens and my own driver, Jack Holway. Courtney knew of Edgar Stephens but not Jack Holway. It was decided that their particular style of driving a steam engine might best be characterised as 'unconventional'. It was always accepted that anyone could 'drive' a locomotive once shown how. But the manner of doing it differed. There were those who 'nursed' the locomotive through skill developed over years and a full understanding as to how a steam engine worked. They would continuously

The mystery solved. 3709 at Truro shed again; before it had come to Cornwall had been at Didcot in Oxfordshire where it was equipped with this spark arrester so it could safely shunt the local Army yards where wagons of ammunition were present. At some point the 'busby' had to be taken off (they could be a nuisance) with the chimney case, presumably, still sat in a corner of the stores back in Didcot. R.C. Riley, www.transporttreasury.co.uk

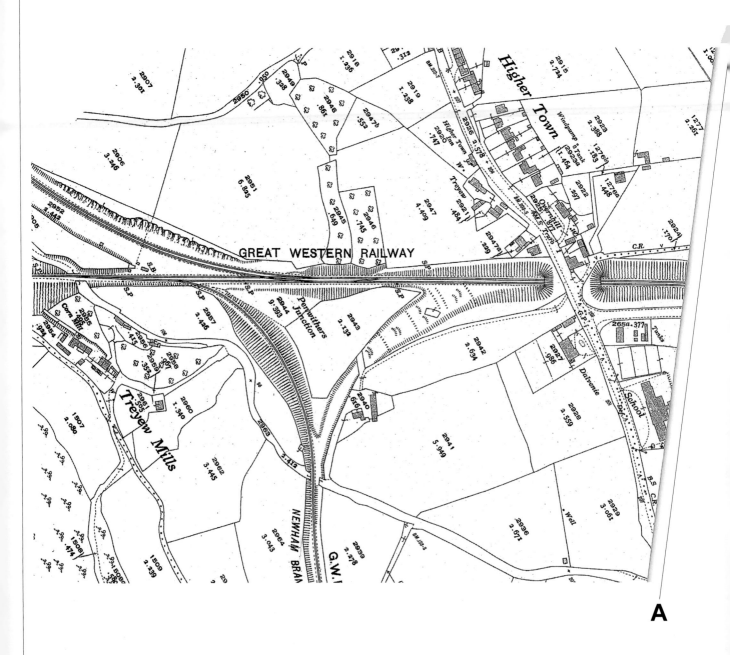

A

A couple of more or less temporary sheds were in use as the railway established itself at Truro. A permanent building came with the arrival of the Cornwall Railway in 1859, a two road timber building with a slate roof. With its coal stage, blacksmiths shop, workshop and water tank, it sufficed until around 1900 when the latter-day shed, which survived to operate briefly as a diesel depot in the 1960s, was built. The locomotive allocations in 1950 was:

4-6-0: 1013 COUNTY OF CORNWALL, 4906 BRADFIELD HALL, 4936 KINLET HALL, 6931 ALDBOROUGH HALL, 6872 CRAWLEY GRANGE
2-6-0: 6373
2-6-2T: 4167, 4504, 4523, 4554, 4561, 4588, 4589, 5500, 5515, 5526, 5537, 5562
0-6-0PT: 1782, 2097, 5779, 7422, 8412

1932

adjust the amount that the regulator was opened, sometimes altering was a slight tap of the fingers either up or down, at the same time watching the blast of the exhaust from the chimney to see the desired result. They would also alter the length of the stroke of the pistons by the use of the reserving lever or screw; adjusting the 'cut-off'. In short they coaxed the best out of their engines using the minimum of effort. The result was less coal burnt, thereby making their fireman's work that much easier.

The opposite was the driver who, in achieving the same results on the road, would do so with the regulator wide open, the stroke of the pistons that much longer, and thereby burning probably half as much coal as the driver described above. These had the nickname of 'hard hitters' though it was never said within their hearing. I hasten to assure the reader that in both cases they were 'masters' of their profession, but we liked to refer to the

Top. Chacewater on 8 April 1960 and Truro's 5515 is standing at the Newquay branch platform with a with a Truro-Newquay passenger train. R.C. Riley, www.transporttreasury.co.uk

Middle. 4587, having brought the afternoon passenger from Newquay as far as Chacewater, restarts from the branch platform there on 17 August 1958, for the final run to Truro. A.E. Bennett, www.transporttreasury.co.uk

Below. Just over twelve miles up the branch from Chacewater was Shepherds. One of the original stations on this line, it dates from 1905. In the height of the boom in mineral mining, Shepherds was an important junction for a branch to mines in the area. Everything is relaxed as the driver of 4587 awaits the 'right away' to get the train moving on the final leg to Newquay.   A.E.   Bennett, www.transporttreasury.co.uk

Above. Trenance Viaduct on the outskirts of Newquay, and on 18 July 1956 2-6-2T 4565 is close to Newquay station with the Truro passenger service. S. Creer, www.transporttreasury.co.uk

Middle. Truro 2-6-2Ts 4167 and 4587 on separate platforms at Newquay station, 17 August 1958, ready to depart with their trains. It is possible that 4167 is working a diagram to Par and then on the main line back to Truro. A.E. Bennett, www.transporttreasury.co.uk

Bottom. Truro station on 14 June 1947 and the Penzance driver waits for the signal to drop to start 1023 COUNTY OF OXFORD with a train for Plymouth. R.C. Riley, www.transporttreasury.co.uk

first one as an 'Engineman' and the second as a 'Driver'. Percy Kimber of St Blazey Shed and Edgar Stephens of Laira, were both renown gentlemen, but I will not place them firmly in either category.

The Jack Holways of the footplate were a different 'breed' altogether. Probably because they did not conform. I fired to Jack and would hasten to state that he was an 'Engineman'. He could get the best possible results with least amount of effort. It was a pleasure to fire for him, the problem was that you were never sure what he was going to do. Again I hasten to reassure that he would never have a disregard for safety. That and the keeping to time was always uppermost. I always believed that he was ahead of his time. He was the nearest thing to a one of the 'flower people' in his manner and outlook before any of them were born. He would love to imitate someone who he had seen on a film in the cinema or had read about in a book. He once arrived wearing the garb of Sherlock Holmes and smoking a large curved stem pipe! What all of these had in common, were that they were 'characters' perhaps something in short supply these days.

At Truro there had been a driver called Ted Solomon. He was regarded as a good engineman, but had some odd ways of working; on one of the daily trip goods, back from Drump Lane, the yard just to the east of Redruth, for instance. The locomotive was invariably a small prairie and once over the top at Chacewater and on the falling gradient to Truro, Ted would drop down on his seat with a sigh that betokened a sense of finality and announce to the fireman that he had 'done his bit'. From now on it was up to the fireman to control the train the remainder of the way home by the engine handbrake. The first time this happened, Courteney got quite apprehensive well, very apprehensive actually to judge from the knocking sound of his knees. On entering Highertown tunnel he was only too aware of the steep drop once the train exited. It was never clear (you just didn't inquire about some things to some drivers) quite what was in Ted's mind; a well

Right. 0-6-0PT 8486 standing in Truro goods yard in the summer of 1958. From left to right: Fireman Courtney Berryman, Head Shunter J. Rushworth, Shunter S. Richards, Driver Vic Elvins. Courtney Berryman.

Middle. A deserted Falmouth station forecourt in May 1960. 5546 shatters the calm over in the branch platform. James Harrold, www.transporttreasury.co.uk

Bottom. Pannier tank 3709 (still missing its chimney casing) from Truro shed shunting her train at Falmouth before departing for Truro goods yard. The water column, tank and engine road are all that is left of the old two road Falmouth engine shed, closed in 1925. R.C. Riley, www.transporttreasury.co.uk

Left. A view out over Falmouth Harbour from Penmere Station with Trefusis Point in the background .

Middle. Goonbell Halt looking towards Chacewater on the line to Newquay, 26 September 1956; the platform was situated just 50 chains from St Agnes station. H.C. Casserley, courtesy R.M. Casserley.

meaning if misguided introduction to the complexities of life on the footplate, or was he just tired? Maybe he was demonstrating his knowledge of the road and his complete control of the loco and train, for he was clearly still keeping an eye on things; as they left the tunnel, to Courtney's enormous relief, Ted abandoned what seconds earlier had seemed a permanent occupancy of the seat and grandly took control.

I had wondered if, having worked from Chacewater to Newquay, did the Truro blokes ever go on then to Par? It seems they did. It was just one turn, booking on at something like 5.0 am to prepare a 45XX or 55XX small prairie, off shed at 5.45 am to work the first passenger train at 6.05 am, Truro to Newquay via Chacewater. Arrival at Newquay was 7.11 am. They had time for breakfast before setting off for Par with the same carriage set at something like 8.15am away from Newquay. There was a quick turn round there with just time to take on water and leave again with a passenger train from Par back to Newquay, and then they finished up with the 11.50 am from Newquay, arriving at Chacewater around 12.40 pm. Leaving the carriage set in the branch platform they returned light engine to Truro. A full day's work but a satisfying one.

The Chacewater-Newquay was another 'roller-coaster' with some

Truro 2-6-2T 4588 is signalled out of the East Junction at Chacewater, running round after working the 11.53am from Newquay, 26 September 1956. H.C. Casserley, courtesy R.M. Casserley.

The west end of Truro shed showing coal stage, water tanks and turntable, 26 September 1956. The shed breakdown vans are in the middle. H.C. Casserley, courtesy R.M. Casserley.

gradients severe enough to make the big prairie 'dig its heels in'; more so than ever in the summer when the carriages were full to standing with passengers. Leaving Chacewater there was a rising gradient of 1 in 45 to Mount Hawke; the line then levelled out to St Agnes before falling to almost sea level at Perranporth. A steep climb then followed up to Goonhavern, with a procession of 'ups and downs' to Shepherds. It was a falling gradient again to Trewerry, with a final pull up to Tolcarn Junction before joining with the Par line for the run into Newquay. A full load for a '45' was 170 tons – something like five coaches.

Of course while nearly every day was a full day, a happy or satisfying one it was not. With driver Bill Cook, Courtney recalled relieving a Laira crew on a special train, carrying equipment for Hayle

power station. The locomotive was a 28XX class 2-8-0 and though perfectly strong enough in one sense it could not have been more ill-suited to the task. The day was very wintry with occasional snow showers, and bitterly cold. The 28XXs were good enough locomotives for any heavy work that might be going and you often felt that they could pull any length and weight of train. In terms of comfort in bad conditions, however, they were more suited to the 1900s than the 1950s. They had a very short cab and offered only the barest protection from the elements.

The train was somewhere near a full load and required a banking engine from Truro goods yard up and through the tunnel at Highertown; the locomotive was steaming reasonably well, and no undue problems were experienced on the run

to Hayle. Shunting the train into the sidings at Hayle, Courtney anticipated a run to Long Rock shed at Penzance to turn the engine before running back to Truro. A cup of tea figured largely in this. Imagine his surprise and dismay when Bill announced that they would run back to Truro light, tender first; the signalman was to be informed so that could release them as soon as maybe. He obviously had some urgent need to get back early, whether at a wife's command or the siren call of the pub. It is difficult to relate just how miserable the ensuing journey was, on into freezing night with no escape, however tightly you jammed yourself in the corner of the cab, as close as you could bear to the hot backplate. Courtney had never been so cold and miserable before or since and almost staggered from the footplate on arrival on shed at Truro.

Another time firing with Bill Cook they relieved a down pick-up goods, slow as a snail and thus universally called the 'snaily'. The loco was a Hall 4-6-0 and a bad 'un, and the job a memorable one for it was the one and only time in Courtney's career that they ran out of steam on the job. Now this is always a fear in the back of any fireman's mind with a poorly steaming engine; we all dreaded having to stop for lack of steam because it was always somehow your fault, even if it wasn't. Worse, with injector failure the level of water in the boiler could fall below a certain level; above the firebox crown was a fusible lead plug, which melted should the crown overheat in the absence of sufficient water. Steam and the remaining water would then rush into the firebox extinguishing the fire. This would prevent the boiler from exploding but might also extinguish your career. The locomotive, of course, would be disabled completely. In Courtney's case it was the poor state of

One of Truro's 94XX 0-6-0PTs, 8485 attached to one of the shunting 'chariots' on 26 September 1956. H.C. Casserley, courtesy R.M. Casserley.

the fire, something that could be overcome with effort and good luck and it was decided to stop the train and give the fireman a chance to liven the fire and raise a bit of steam by getting some of the clinker off the firebars. The stop lasted some fifteen minutes, and he was able to put things right (sort of) and continue onwards. Of course, this did not end the matter for on booking off the required report into the why and wherefore of his actions had to be made in the foremans office.

The Newham branch ran 2½ miles from Penwithers Junction off the Falmouth branch, forming a steeply falling 'U' shaped line and curving around the south-west high ground of the city to the wharf alongside the Truro River. Truro shed worked two goods a day in and out of Newham, with a 45XX small prairie. The first was mainly coal for the gas works, loaded in and empties out. The second was a general mix of goods; all sorts of items that would be needed, again loaded in and generally empties out, though there would be an occasional loaded wagon taken out; equipment to be repaired and so on. One day Courtney was on the turn and it was very wet. As they eased down the bank the 45XX started to slip on the wet rail; they sanded the rails but the train was moving faster and faster, the brake ineffective. Not knowing what else could be done, Courtney got out on the steps of the engine and jumped down to the ground. As the train was going past he slipped the handbrakes on the wagons out of their safe position to let the brake blocks drag against the wheels, and 'pinned' them down as much as he could. He said that

this had the desired effect and brought the train back under control. As I have often remarked, there was more to being a fireman than just shovelling coal!

The Falmouth branch continued in a virtually straight alignment after the junction with the Newham line. On a rising gradient of 1 in 66 for approximately a mile, the line reached the position of the original Penwithers Viaduct which was a Brunel timber structure resting on masonry piers. It was 271 yards in length and 90 feet in height. In 1926 the viaduct was replaced, though legend has it that it is in fact still *in situ* within the embankment. After this comes the 300 yard Penwithers cutting and then only a short distance on, the first tunnel at Sparnick, some 490 yards in length. The tunnel marked the top of the incline and the line then fell steeply towards Perranwell, to a viaduct at Carnon, 252 yards long and 96 feet high. Leaving Perranwell the line climbed to Perran Tunnel, about 400 yards long, on a rising gradient of something like 1 in 60, but levelled out at the approach. After the tunnel the next structure was the viaduct at Ponsanooth, among the highest in Cornwall. From Ponsanooth the track passed through a deep cutting at Roskrow Hill, before falling steeply to Penryn. There was a falling gradient then to Collegewood viaduct, at 318 yards the longest on the Falmouth branch and the last of Brunel's timber viaducts in use. From Collegewood the line started to climb once more to Penmere and then fell sharply towards the station at Falmouth.

'And that's it'! pronounced Courtney. Not quite, I thought and asked him about

the trains over the branch. It was pretty busy, it turned out, with something like sixteen passenger trains a day in the summer, and two daily goods trains. The passenger service included a 'through' train departing for London at 9.30 in the morning, and one from London arriving at 4.30 pm. Two passenger trains were extended to Newquay. The docks at Falmouth, which had its own diesel shunter, such was the level of work, provided most of the goods traffic on the branch, though there was local trade as well. This was mostly fertiliser and coal though there were wagons of sugar beet for the United Biscuits premises at Perranwell, and oil tankers for Penryn. Cattle from the local markets left on the branch, from lineside pens at Penryn.

There was an unusual turn at Truro in which, on booking on at 3.45 am, they had first to 'prep' three 45XX 2-6-2Ts before taking one of them to work the Falmouth goods. The other two engines were for passenger trains to Falmouth and Newquay. It was a pleasure talking with Courtney and I am grateful to him and for the lore he imparted.

Shepherds up platform, looking south on 31 May 1960. L.R. Freeman, www.transporttreasury.co.uk

When the old shed near the station became all-too obviously inadequate, land was procured at Long Rock and a new engine shed, opening in 1914. A typical Churchward straight shed with four roads it is unusual to see such buildings, normally smoky, dirty and cluttered, in this 'as new' condition. The place could only have opened that day, or week.

Chapter 8
Penzance Engine Shed and Workings

St Ives to St. Erth

St Erth on the main line to lovely St Ives clinging to the cliffs has the distinction of being the last length of the old broad gauge (7ft ¼in) track to be converted to 'narrow' or standard gauge, 4ft 8½in, in 1892. It was the almost exclusive domain of the 45XX 2-6-2Ts from Penzance shed, usually with a two or three carriage load, although on a Saturday in the summer season this could be increased to four or even six. The highlight of the summer was the Saturday only working of the through portion of the Cornish Riviera Express which needed double-heading in both directions over the branch, with two 45XXs on the front and occasionally one at the rear too. From St Erth the line fell to sea level at Lelant, then rose to Carbis Bay station before another drop of 1in 44 on the steepest length towards St Ives.

Passenger Train Schedules Summer Saturday 1957

St Erth dep.	St Ives arr.	Originated from
05.18 Light engine	05.30	Penzance Shed.
06.02	06.18	20.12 ex Paddington
06.35	06.53	Local
07.48	08.00	Local
08.40	08.57	08.25 ex-Penzance
09.36	09 50	Local
10.20	10.34	Local
11.17	11.32	Local
12.05	12.20	Local
12.25	12.40	Local
13.30	13.45	Local
14.15	14.30	Local
14.45	15.00	Local
15.10	15.25	Local
15.55	16.10	Local
16.40	16.55	Local
17.15	17.35	10.30 ex-Paddington
18.25	18.40	Local
18.50	19.05	Local
19.35	19.50	Local
21.15	21.30	Local
21.45	22.00	Local

St Ives dep.	St Erth arr.	Destination
05.45	06.00	Local
06.55.Empty Stock	07.05	Penzance
07.25	07.40	Local
08.10	08.25	Local
09.20 Cornish Riviera	09.35	Paddington
09.55	10.10	Local
10.40	10.55	Local
10.55	11.10	Local
11.40	11.55	Local
13.05	13.20	Local
13.50	14.05	Local
14.35 Empty Stock	14.45	St Erth(Loco to PZ)
15.30	15. 45	Local
16.20	16.35	Local
17.45	18.00	Local
18.05	18.20	Local
19.10	19.25	Local
19.55	20.10	Local
20.35	20.50	Local
21.20	21.35	Local
22.10 Empty Stock	22.25	St Erth

Gwinear Road to Helston
8miles 67 chains

The branch opened in 1887 and there were grand ideas for an extension through to the Lizard, to rival the established holiday resorts of South Devon, Torbay in particular. Shortly after the junction with the main line at Gwinear Road, the line climbed for 2¼ miles to the first station at Praze, which was also close to the village of Crowan. Praze had a platform with water tower at the north end, a small yard and a goods loop. The points were operated from a ground frame, with the keys connected with the single line token. From Praze the line continued on a falling gradient of 1 in 60 at its steepest before reaching Nancegollan. This station was in the heart of farm country, and was a centre for the despatch of early flowers, broccoli and potatoes. To meet this growing trade the station and goods yard was enlarged in 1937. After Nancegollan the line went through a series of cuttings and embankments to Truthull halt. The arrangements were sparse, a wooden platform and a typical GWR corrugated iron 'pagoda' waiting shelter. The section on to Helston just over two miles off was noted for its varying curves. From Cober viaduct there was a short rising gradient to the station. The Helston branch, though perhaps never in the headlines as a particularly popular holiday resort, at least not in comparison with say, St Ives, Newquay and Looe, nevertheless the line warranted an additional four workings on a summer Saturday. In addition, through express passenger trains, including the prestigious Cornish Riviera, were scheduled to stop at Gwinear Road station to make connection. A 'special operating instruction' stipulated that the 1.35 pm Helston to Gwinear Road 'Must Not Be Delayed' and was to be given 'Special Attention'. Arrival time at Gwinear Road was critical to connect with through services, which, if delayed, could have a 'knock-on' effect on the whole time table, even including the 'Royal Duchy' no less!

Passenger Train Schedule Summer Saturday 1958

Helston dep.	Gwinear Road arr.	Gwinear Road dep.	Helston arr.
05.45	06.10	06.15	06.40
07.45	08.12	08.35	09.00
09.45	10.10	10.15	10.44
10.20	10.45	10.50	11.15
11.50	12.15	12.37	13.02
13.15	13.40	13.48	14.12
15.20	15.47	15.55	16.20
16.35	17.05	17.24	17.50
18.05	18.35	18.55	19.24
19.25	19.48	19.50	20.14
20.35	21.02	21.30	21.55.

Hayle Wharf Branch 55 chains

Hayle was a major port for the export of copper ore from the Redruth and Camborne area and in particular from the Crofty and Roskear mines. The ore was originally brought to Hayle wharves by packhorses and mules until the West Cornwall Railway, having re-routed a section of main line to avoid the inclines at Penponds and Angarrack, constructed a new line with a falling gradient of 1 in 30 for the length of 300 yards or so from the new station at Hayle. In addition to the trade in copper ore the wharves also served an explosives works situated in the adjacent sand dunes, and the local foundry at Hayle. Shunting at the wharves was carried out by horses and Penzance shed worked a daily train to the wharves hauled by either a small prairie or pannier tank. The ships which served this industry brought in coal for the mining industry as well as scrap iron for the foundry. As many as 30 wagons could be propelled at one time along the wharf with the brake van leading. However, propelling was not allowed once the bottom of the incline was reached. In addition, the loading had to be greatly reduced for the journey up the incline; it called for some nifty train handling by the Penzance men. The little Hayle Wharf line closed in 1983.

I am fascinated by this odd little line; Leslie Hunt (see below) when it was mentioned smiled – 'sand boxes', he remarked. With that gradient it was critical that they were working and full. Trains could be heavy, with sulphur for an ICI plant, closed vans for the dynamite works (always glad to take your leave of these!), petrol tankers and equipment for the electric power station. That short line 'tested everything', train handling, brakes, couplings and steaming.

****

Looking into the work of Penzance shed, I encountered a fairly fundamental stumbling block, in that I couldn't find a single former driver or fireman from whom I could obtain some personal

The Harbour at Penzance with the 'dog-leg' pier to protect the craft inside from the storms. In the mid 1800s this area would have been full of trawlers. The pilchard shoals from July onwards absolutely filled Mounts bay and they were followed by the herring. After that came the mackerel.

The present day boats venture further out to sea in an effort to find the diminishing stocks. Unheard of at one time, the huge trawlers from Lowestoft and Grimsby began to cast their nets in the traditionally Cornish waters.

The rear of the shed in July 1914, with some of its first occupants inside. The view shows how the ground was made up to accommodate the structure.

The spacious interior with immaculate residents in 1914. To the right is 4-4-0 3379 RIVER FAL, with two more 4-4-0s alongside including 3345 SMEATON. The coach-like vehicle on the left bears the number 63 and would be one of the steam railmotors built about a decade before.

The last of these photographs of the Penzance Long Rock shed when new, shows the impressive coal stage, capped by a 45,000 gallon water tank.

From the coal stage, looking east. The shed yard lay alongside the old A30 (almost deserted on 9 April 1960!) and from left to right can be identified 6824 ASHLEY GRANGE, pannier 1650 and standing by the coal wagon with a full head of steam 1018 COUNTY OF LEICESTER. R.C. Riley, www.transporttreasury.co.uk

stories. I did the rounds (purely in the interests of research you understand) of the local hostelries likely to be frequented by retired railwaymen with no success. However from one of the advertisements placed in the local newspapers, I at last had some luck. I received an e-mail from Roger Salter who, as a young lad regularly visited the shed, 'train spotting' and taking down engine numbers. He was able to introduce me to Jack Mathews, a former Penzance railwayman, in the Traffic Department. Jack was known from writings in certain railway publications, and as a result of speaking with him, I received the name and telephone number of a former Penzance shed man, Leslie Hunt.

I met with Les, his charming wife, and son, a railwayman now himself, in Penzance and spent a very fruitful couple of hours listening, and taking notes. He had been 'born into the railway', as we said in those days, at Newton Abbot in Devon where his father, Wilfred Norman Hunt, was a boilersmith. His uncle Walter was also a boilersmith, firstly at Newton Abbot and then at Taunton, who had joined the railway at Penzance as a shunter, before moving to Manchester. In 1930 when Les was a very young lad, his parents moved from Newton Abbot to Penzance when his father was transferred there.

Les duly started as a cleaner boy at Long Rock engine shed in February 1945, and in 1946 was made fireman, taking up the first available vacancy, at Taunton shed. As most of us did, he immediately placed his name on the list for transfer

back to his 'home' shed as and when a vacancy arose. This was slow in coming; he was called up for National Service in 1947, serving in an Infantry regiment both in England and in Germany. Completing his army service in 1949 he returned to Taunton to find that whilst he was away the wheels of staffing movements had continued to turn, and that he had been transferred back home *in absentia* as it were! He was finally made a driver at Penzance in 1963, with steam extinguished. His drivers examination was conducted by a panel which included Inspector Cook, so well known as a former foreman at Laira.

Les unfortunately had to retire early in 1992 due to ill-health, but even so he had given the railway 47½ years of loyal service. He was emphatic that the in early days and under the Great Western Railway, it was in his own words, 'a lovely job and a job for life'. He was not impressed with the changes that came with nationalisation. The decline of steam in the period leading up to its complete replacement by diesels was particularly hard to stomach. At Penzance it was not so bad as was seen later in the 1960s in other parts of the country but once-coddled locomotives became miserably run down for lack of attention. The changeover from steam to diesel had saddened him; 'You see' he said, 'steam locomotives lived. There was always movement in them even when stationary as long as they were in steam. Diesels died when you switched them off. They were lifeless. Nothing to relate to or to get attached to.'

As with so many others, he was of the opinion that the railway was used as a 'political pawn' and that the losers were the railway itself and those that worked upon it. He recalled the bitter dispute between ASLEF and BR in 1955, and how it had started out of a 'difference between a fireman and a guard'! The eventual result was a settlement which seemed to have no bearing on the original complaint; drivers received an extra 2/6d a week, and firemen exactly nothing! The loss of business to road lorries accelerated after this ruinous dispute and was irrecoverable, ending in the loss of almost all goods traffic.

In happier times Les recalled a trip on an old friend of mine, 4906 BRADFIELD HALL, formerly of Truro shed, but transferred in the later days of steam to Penzance. They had worked her up to Plymouth with the midnight goods, the 'owl', as it was known and near to Scorrier an already out of sorts 4906 started to steam badly. The arrow on the steam gauge started to fall steadily backwards, and the water level in the boiler was lowering significantly. Les got the fire iron out of the rack on the tender and levelled the fire over the box, at the same time looking for a reason for the failing fire. At times a 'hole' would develop in it, allowing cold air up through the firebars. Levelling the fire would normally have the desired result, but no such luck this time. He felt sure that the cause was not clinker forming on the firebars, the fall off of steam had happened too suddenly; it had to be a mechanical fault.

Small prairie 4552 is on coal stage shunt duties, bringing down the empty coal wagons to be placed in the sidings to then collect probably four or five fully loaded ones and push them up the ramp until the leading wagon reaches the buffer stops. Then, after ensuring that all the handbrakes are securely pinned down, 4552 can drop to the bottom of the ramp. Coalmen manage the wagons themselves once they are up in place. As they become empty the men will control forward movement with the hand brakes, moving the empties forward to permit the next two laden ones to come into the working area. R.C. Riley, www.transporttreasury.co.uk

On the coal stage road 6938 CORNDEAN HALL waits for coaling and fire cleaning; the smokebox will be cleared of ashes and these will be shovelled into the 'firepit' to join the fire clinker. Later the whole lot will be shovelled back out, then shovelled into a wagon for disposal. A good job labour was cheap! C.Howsom/R Parkes.

PENZANCE ENGINE SHED 1933

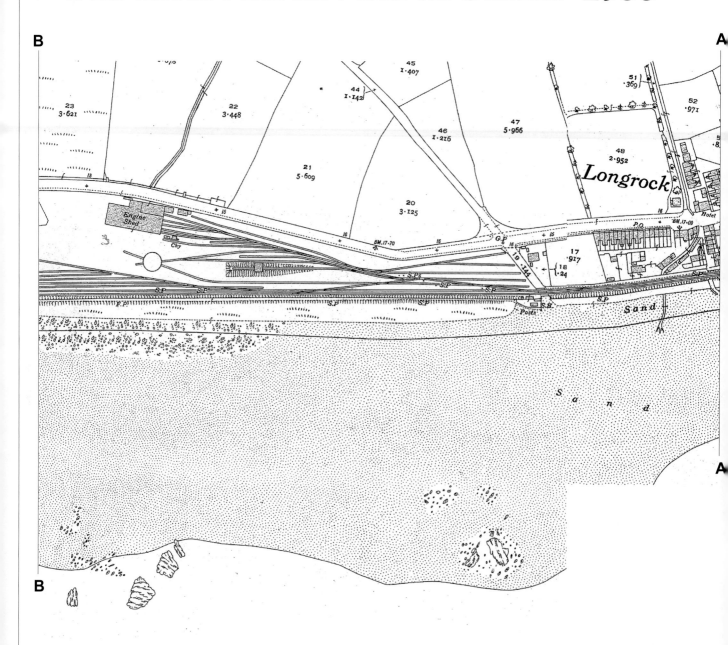

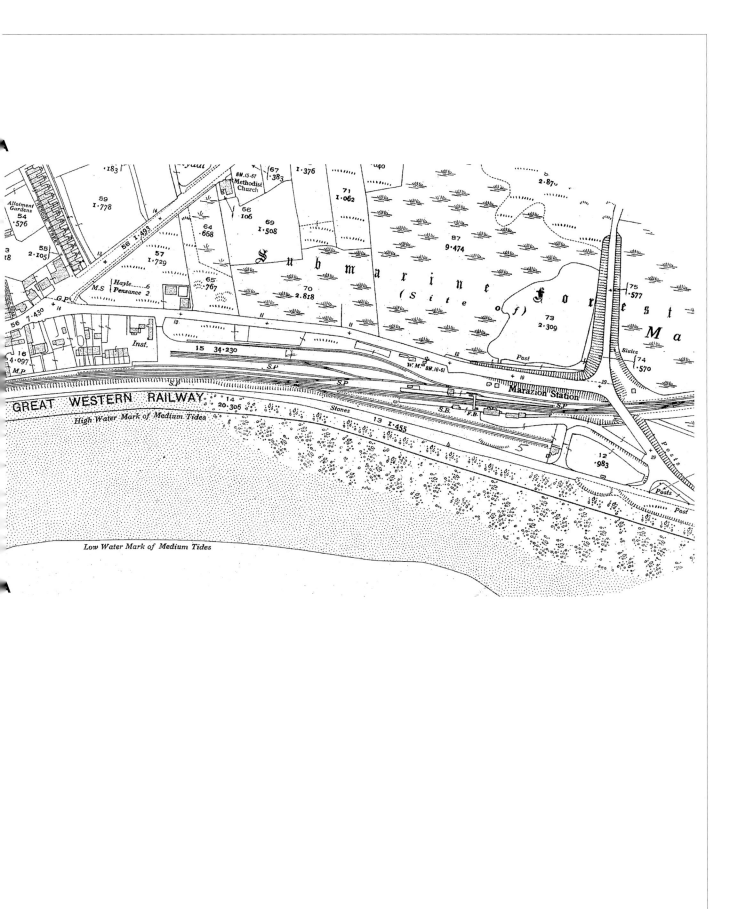

PENZANCE STATION 1933

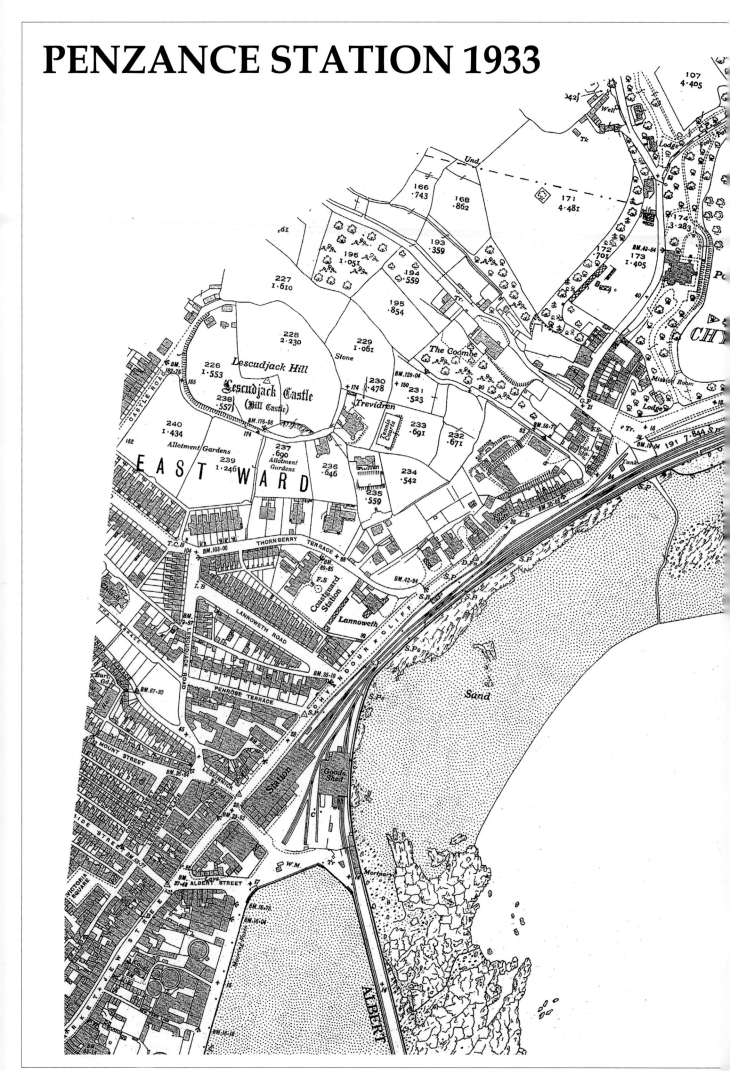

C

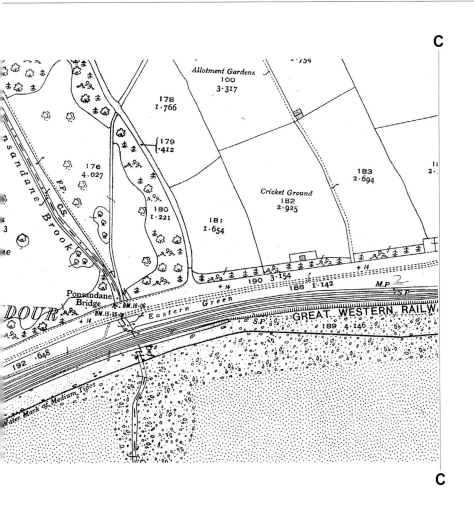

Allotment Gardens
100
3·317

178
1·766

179
·412

176
4·027

183
2·694

180
1·221

181
1·654

Cricket Ground
182
2·925

190 3·154

188 1·142

M.P 2
S.P

Ponsandane Bridge
BM.16·06
BM.15·95
Eastern Green

DOUR

GREAT WESTERN RAILW·

S.P

189 4·146

192 ·648

Water Mark of Medium Tides

C

B

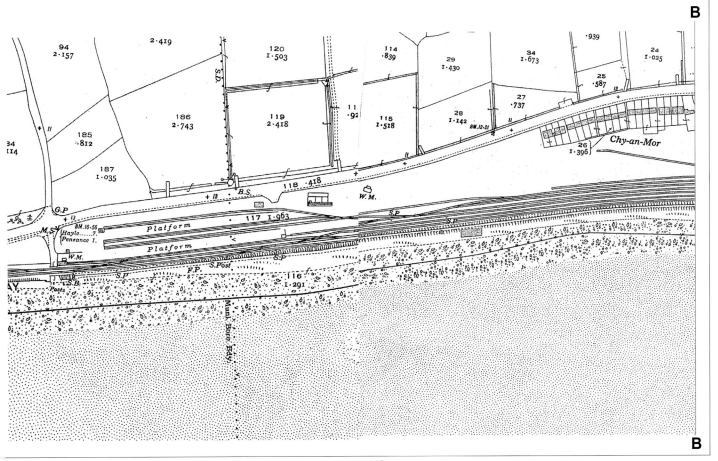

94
2·157

2·419

120
1·503

114
·839

29
1·430

34
1·673

·939

24
1·025

S.D.

25
·587

186
2·743

119
2·418

11
·92

115
1·518

28
1·142

27
·737

BM.12·21

26
1·396

Chy-an-Mor

185
·812

187
1·035

118 ·418

B.S.

W.M.

G.P
M.S
BM.16·56
Hayle....7.
Penzance 1.

Platform

117 1·963

S.P

S.P

Platform

W.M.

S.P

F.P. S.Post

S.P

Posts

116
1·291

·AY

S.B.

S.P

Mun. Boro Bdy.

The driver stopped the train at Scorrier and with the blower put on to prevent a back draught on the footplate, Les went around to the front end and opened the smoke box door. His immediate inspection showed all to be in order. The tubes were clean with no sign of any water or steam leaks. The baffle plate was in place and the jumper ring appeared secure in its normal position. But Les had an instinct about that jumper ring. This piece of ironmongery sat atop of the blast pipe and would lift and drop according to how hard the locomotive was working. Hard at it and the ring lifts, opening additional 'ports' (holes) to permit the exhaust steam a greater opening to escape up the chimney. Returning to the cab to arm himself with the coal pick Les climbed back to the smokebox and gave the ring a sharp whack and found that it was firmly stuck – thereby the cause of the trouble. Tapping the ring on all sides eventually freed it from the char that had 'welded' it to the blast pipe. This done Les returned to the footplate, and finding the steam pressure and water now returned to normal with the enforced stop, his driver informed the guard and signalman that they were able to proceed with the train. All firemen at some stage have to handle steaming problems. The usual solution, though undertaken only reluctantly, was to stop for a 'blow up'. The uncomfortable aftermath, unless it could be discreetly overlooked, was normally a 'report' to appease the 'higher-ups'.

Les was once asked to work the 10.15 pm potato special to Truro and on arriving there was somewhat peeved to find that the last train back to Penzance had already gone, which meant spending the night in Truro. The night foreman there suggested that he catch the Kensington parcels, departing Truro at something like 6.0 am. The parcel vans of course had no seating, comfy or otherwise and a jolting ride on the floor of a parcels van held very few attractions. The journey would also be interminable, for the parcels stopped everywhere for dropping off and also to let the early morning traffic overtake it. To Les it was clear; he'd be better off catching the night sleeper at 6.30 am and ride home to Penzance in relative comfort. What is more the sleeper would arrive in Penzance 45 minutes earlier that the parcels. This done he eventually booked off duty having worked a total of 16 hours and 10 minutes. This was in direct contravention of an instruction given that no one was to work more than twelve hours on any one shift; handily for 'the company' (BR of course) this meant that that he was obliged to go without pay for his pains – beyond the twelve hours at least. He could sing for it.

Two weeks later Les was on a morning 'spare' turn when the Laira fireman on the down early morning passenger was taken ill and carted off to hospital. Les was required to step up and fire the 12.30 up passenger to Plymouth with the Laira driver. On coupling on to the train, Les

was returning to the footplate when he noticed some senior officers, about to board the train, in conference on the platform near the cab. At that one of the officials left the group and approached Les, enquiring if he was the Penzance fireman. Now this person was the originator of the very 12 hour directive and the cause of his discomfiture over the money he considered due to him. So Les was less than overwhelmed to be told he was a 'good lad' to step into the breach. It was pointed out somewhat forcefully to the 'bowler hat' that by doing so, by the time he arrived back from Plymouth, hopefully on the Swansea, he would have worked well over the stipulated 12 hours and not get paid for his pains.

Yet this was quite alright, dear chap; after all, was not seeing to the train and passengers 'above all other considerations'? For Les, his moment had arrived; he looked the man responsible for depriving him of four hours and ten minutes of overtime in the eye and recounted his thankless efforts of a few weeks before. Was there not some illogicality at work here? His actual words of were rather different and as forceful and Anglo Saxon as a senior official is ever likely to hear. Perhaps the observance of these edicts was dependent on who was travelling on the train? Again, it was rather less polite than that. He turned on his heel and stomped back to the footplate. The senior official pondered long, eventually choosing to understate

Sign of the times. SWITHLAND HALL and TRELLECH GRANGE with D833 showing its front end on 24 September 1960. R.C. Riley, www.transporttreasury.co.uk

A sight to warm the heart of any steam enthusiast; locomotives in pristine condition with the newness of 'shopping' replaced by the sheen of the cleaners' oily cotton waste. From nearest the camera on 24 September 1960 they are: 6824 ASHLEY GRANGE of Penzance, 4920 DUMBLETON HALL from Newton Abbot, 6828 TRELLECH GRANGE of Truro and 6988 SWITHLAND HALL from Laira. R.C. Riley, www.transporttreasury.co.uk

7916 MOBBERLEY HALL on the turntable at Penzance, 29 April 1961. The 'weight' on the turntable relied upon even balance. The driver and his mate and a willing A.N. Other can be seen by the tender pushing heartily on the turntable levers. R.C. Riley, www.transporttreasury.co.uk

where Les had perhaps overstated: 'I seem to have dropped a clanger' he said.

Les had a special memory of driving the restored Great Western 4-4-0 3440 CITY OF TRURO at the head of a Westward Television special down through Cornwall, while another favourite had been Laira's 5028 LLANTILIO CASTLE when newly outshopped and riding like a dream, everything working like a good watch.

We leave Penzance with Les running into the station. Getting down to the platform to watch the passengers go by, he noticed a couple of ladies coming from the train, one pushing a pram, chatting happily away. A glance in the pram revealed it, surprisingly, to be empty. Les remarked to the ladies that was so: 'Oh! my God' was the reaction. 'My baby , my baby, I've left her in the compartment.' And with that she went running back down the platform. All in a days work!

Les Hunt died in October 2010 and sadly will not see his stories in print. Not only did he give me invaluable help but, with his wife Florence, was a delight to talk to. This Chapter is dedicated to his memory.

The cleaner lads at Penzance could certainly turn out a locomotive, especially if it was one of their own. 6800 ARLINGTON GRANGE on 29 April 1961 certainly was a 'favourite son' having been shedded at Penzance from new. R.C. Riley, www.transporttreasury.co.uk

1008 COUNTY OF CARDIGAN on 29 April 1961; behind is another County and, in the background, one of the new North British Type 2 diesel hydraulics, which were to prove disappointing. R.C. Riley, www.transporttreasury.co.uk

Top. Engines need enginemen to make them perform. On 9 April 1960 Penzance's Driver Leonard Rail sits comfortably and contemplatively in the cab at St Erth waiting for the 'right away'. R.C. Riley, www.transporttreasury.co.uk

Middle. St Ives station on 24 September 1960; Drivers Holloway and Ralph standing by their 45XX 2-6-2T. R.C. Riley, www.transporttreasury.co.uk

Left. Without this gentleman it would not have been possible to describe the work of Penzance shed. Repeated pleas for information went unanswered until former 'spotter' Roger Salter put me in contact with Jack Mathews, a great writer of articles in the various journals, who in turn found former Penzance Driver Les Hunt, and it was my lucky day. I have given mention to his contribution to this book in the text. Florence Hunt.

Laira's 6821 LEATON GRANGE runs into Penzance station with a down 'stopping' service on 13 July 1956. When the passengers have departed, LEATON GRANGE will propel the train to the carriage sidings and then go to the shed to turn for the return journey. S. Creer, www.transporttreasury.co.uk

Penzance station on 15 July 1958 and two Western National buses wait for the arrival of a train. When climbing a steep Cornish hill fully laden it was not unknown to find the water in the radiator and cooling system was boiling, and the bus would have to wait to cool down or for cold water to be fetched from a nearby stream. A. Swain, www.transporttreasury.co.uk

Penzance station and Newton Abbot's 4955 PLASPOWER HALL has arrived with the 7.35am 'stopping' service from Newton Abbot, 12 May 1959. The passengers and their luggage now discharged, the locomotive propels the empty stock back to the carriage sidings. Once the carriages are gone, the crew will take their locomotive to Long Rock and after turning and carrying out normal oil and water replenishment, will no doubt also give attention to the 'inner man' before proceeding back to the station for their return working. Michael Mensing.

While it was mainly a 'bucket and spade' clientele, the St Ives branch conjured up images of painters, poets, sculptors and suchlike; young people 'ahead of their time'... From St Erth for most of its length the line ran parallel to the coast, giving passengers views of great beauty. Dr Ian C. Allen, www.transporttreasury.co.uk.

4564 stands in the branch platform at St Erth, waiting to depart with for St Ives. R.C. Riley, www.transporttreasury.co.uk

On 17 August 1958 another Penzance small prairie, 4570, runs into St Ives station, the fireman reaching out to pass the Single Line Working token to the waiting signalman. A.E. Bennett, www.transporttreasury.co.uk

Having reversed the coaching stock to clear the cross-over, 4570 runs with a rumble of wheels and a whiff of smoke around the carriages to couple up again to what will be the front for the return journey to St Erth, 17 August 1958. R.C. Riley, www.transporttreasury.co.uk

Train is ready to depart on time for St Erth, 30 May 1960. James Harrold, www.transporttreasury.co.uk

Above. Departure time 24 September 1960, with 4564. Looks like some of those 'ahead of their time' young people on the platform... R.C. Riley, www.transporttreasury.co.uk

Left. Definitely without anybody 'ahead of their time', a picturesque view of old St Ives taken from a side street. Not a train in sight but the church tower is that of St John in the Fields, the bells of which the author has rung on more than one occasion.

On 18 August 1958 the driver of Prairie tank 4577 is in conversation with a lady on the platform at Gwinear Road. By the smoke coming from the chimney, departure time must be imminent, and the fireman has paid all necessary attention to the fire. The lady sat on the seat is presumably waiting for a main line train, and is sadly showing little interest in what is happening behind. A.E. Bennett, www.transporttreasury.co.uk

The countryside around Helston and Cober Viaduct. It is said to have been the heaviest engineering undertaking on the Helston branch. Built with granite quarried locally, it had six arches and was 373 yards in length. At the highest point it stands 90 feet high and the total cost was given as £6,000. James Harrold, www.transporttreasury.co.uk

4563 on arrival at Helston with a train from Gwinear Road, 30 May 1960. It would appear that the fireman has just uncoupled in order for the loco to run round the train and has taken the headlamp from the bunker and placed it on the front splasher for the return journey. James Harrold, www.transporttreasury.co.uk

Helston station, splendidly deserted between trains, 30 May 1960. James Harrold, www.transporttreasury.co.uk

4563 shunting at Helston, 30 May 1960. There was long a healthy business in agricultural produce and there were always plenty of vans to be seen. Sadly the most lucrative loads were easily undercut when the practice of taking the stuff by road took hold amongst local farmers. One of the factors was that produce went direct by lorry from the farm to the destination; straight away the separate legs, to the local goods yard and to the market at the other end, were eliminated. And on it went. James Harrold, www.transporttreasury.co.uk

After shunting, 4563 is made ready for departure with the 3.30pm for Gwinear Road, on 30 May 1960. James Harrold, www.transporttreasury.co.uk

WR 45XX 2-6-2T 5541 turns at the Southern Region shed at Launceston in May 1961. In the background is the Great Western shed officially closed some years earlier when Western men were transferred across to the Southern side. The old stone built GWR shed survived rather better than the SR's corrugated iron affair, as is plain to see! R.C. Riley, www.transporttreasury.co.uk

A variety of wagons being assembled at Wadebridge in 1962 - note behind the considerable stacks of engine coal. R.C. Riley, www.transporttreasury.co.uk

Chapter 9
Wadebridge Engine Shed

Those who know me will be alarmed that, in my old age, I may have become un-hinged, but suffice it to say at this time that yes, I am aware that this was a *Southern* shed! All will become clear…

The Southern Railway in North Cornwall and West Devon

The Southern Railway had an extensive network in North Cornwall and Devon. Many of the locos came from the big modern shed at Exmouth Junction but there were a number of subsidiary sheds dotted about, principally Barnstaple Junction right up in North Devon and Friary near to our own Laira shed, in Plymouth. The most important SR shed (almost the only shed) in Cornwall was Wadebridge at one of the extremities of the Southern's North Cornwall lines – the fabled 'Withered Arm' of which more later.

Wadebridge was small compared to many GWR sheds in Cornwall, for the levels of traffic were much lower. Yet there were fourteen sets of enginemen at Wadebridge in the 1950s, together with all of the associated labourers and tradesmen. Wadebridge had work from the little port and holiday town of Padstow (then known for catching fish, not cooking them) in the far west to Exmouth Junction in the east; this meant running through

the GW St David's station to just beyond the Southern's Central station on the SR main line proper. In addition to passenger and freight on this route Wadebridge had clay trains off the mineral line from Boscarne Junction to Wenford Bridge.

There were three sections over which both 'companies' – the Western and Southern Regions – had running powers over the lines of the other; Boscarne Junction to Wadebridge and Padstow, Exeter St David's to Cowley Bridge Junction, and, though this did not affect Wadebridge men, Mount Gould Junction to Devonport Junction in the Plymouth area.

****

Howard James, a volunteer fireman on the preserved Bodmin and Wenford Railway, was able to put me in touch with two of his colleagues, also working on that line, who were Southern Region footplatemen in steam days. I met with them in the mess room at Bodmin, and I had a most enjoyable and rewarding couple of hours listening to them, as well as being treated to a true Cornish pasty for my lunch. Courtney Berryman was a fireman at Truro shed and I have included his recollections in Chapter 7. The other person in the mess that day was Tony Hallworth, once a fireman at Wadebridge shed. And this shed of course was

Southern. Nevertheless I was brought up right and proper and recall my parents teaching, that before I departed this mortal life I should attempt to carry out at least one *Christian and Charitable Act.* So I have stifled my natural and better instincts and place on paper something of our conversation. I believe it only truthful to state that for Tony it was just as painful to have his stories told by a Western man!

I knew from Laira days that, though we affected to pity the Southern men (and most non-Laira Western men, let's face it) for their inferior locomotives and primitive practices this was almost entirely banter and mickey-taking of a sort that was then part of life in all workplaces. How did the Southern and the Western Region footplatemen regard each other? It turns out that they were in daily contact, the WR men working round to Wadebridge from Bodmin. They got on perfectly well together in fact and the trains and locomotives they worked were similar. At Laira we were naturally a bit aloof because most of us never had occasion to work in any close sense with the Southern. In Cornwall and North Devon it was different; here trains ran on each others lines and sheds and mess rooms were shared, daily. Wadebridge was not the only 'point of contact' by any means. Apart from Exeter for instance,

Replacements for the Beattie well tanks, one of the 'dockie' pannier tanks 1369. They had been taken off Weymouth Quay duties and transferred to this Cornish outpost.

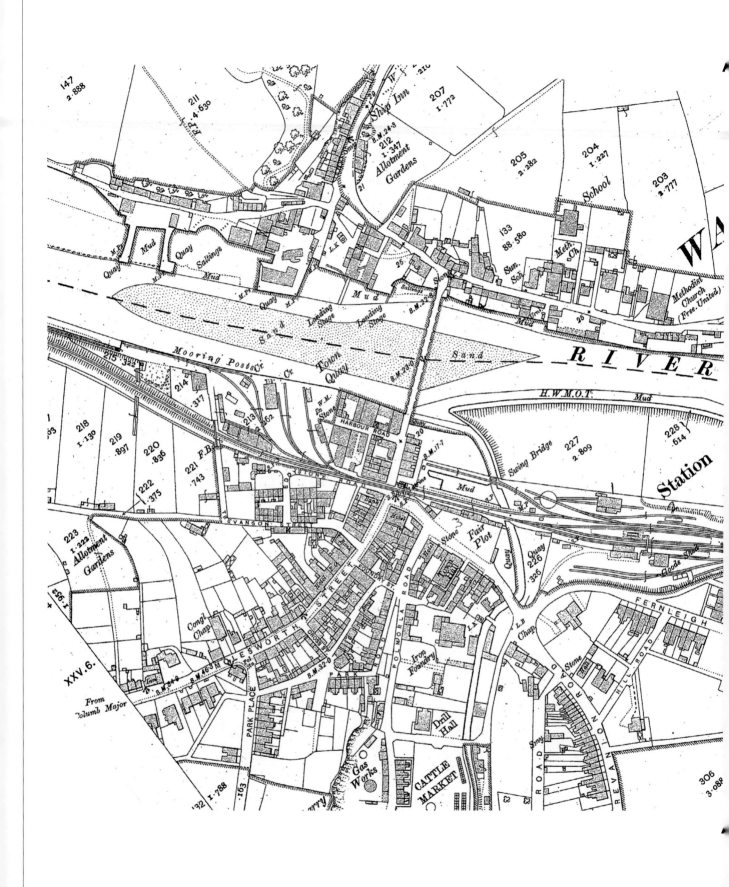

at Launceston the Southern and Western had stations side by side as well as engine sheds and turntables. The usual banter was just that, and jibes, comments and jokes masked a depth of respect between railwaymen whatever their ostensible allegiance, something that it was not possible for either to admit or give credit to when face to face. It never ends of course; with a grin Tony Hallworth enquired if I was aware that the 'S' in SR, actually stood for *Superior*. I of course did not, and in thanking him for this revelation, felt obliged to enlighten him in turn. Did he know that, to all right-thinking people, the two initials SR actually meant *Swindon Reject*?

Tony mourned the closure of the Southern shed at Launceston. It had resulted in a somewhat ridiculous working, whereby the Southern men ran light engine from Wadebridge to Launceston to shunt the Southern goods yard and then returned light all the way back to Wadebridge. He was less than enthusiastic about the Western 1366 class 0-6-0PTs which had replaced the ageing Beattie well tanks. They were not regarded as comparable with the old LSWR 2-4-0WTs and were rough riding. This may well have been so, for the panniers were stop-gaps at best and they in turn had had a long life. Fortunately speeds were exceedingly low! Again, I had to recall the injunctions of my loving parents. All thought of any rejoinder – perhaps the Southern men were unused

to such excellently designed and constructed engines – was instantly banished from my mind.

Tony had started his working life on the Southern Region at Wadebridge shed in 1960 and enthused over the Wenford branch. A trip on a 'Beattie' up that wooded valley for some five or six miles was like a ride on a private railway, a different world. His description recalled for me my early days on the Yealmpton branch, described in *Laira Fireman*. The line commenced just east of Boscarne Junction, between Bodmin General and Wadebridge, and was originally constructed to bring 'sea sand' from the Camel estuary for use as soil improver on the farms in the Helland area. Wagons returned, handily, laden with clay from the Stannon pits. Later on, when the days of using sea sand for farmland were over, empty clay wagons went up in the morning. There were also vans for bagged clay.

A 'travelling shunter' went with the train in addition to a guard and upon arriving at Boscarne Junction one of them would get the key to unlock the points for the branch from the signal box. The train would then proceed on to the branch, with the points promptly re-set for the through line and the key returned to the box. As Tony put it, 'we were locked in'. Unusually for a single line, there was no tablet or token issued. The gradients were not steep and the track was almost level going. There were a

number of severe curves as the line wound its way through the woods; this had a peculiar 'drag' effect, the cumulative friction effectively adding tons to weight of the train; it was as if brakes were being partially applied. Along with this was the excessive squealing noise from those tortured flanges, protesting as they ground against the steel of the rails.

There were ungated road crossings at Dunmere and Helland where the train had to come to a stand and the engine whistle sounded repeatedly. The guard stood in the middle of the road and waved a red flag as warning to motorists, and once clear the train could proceed on its way across the highway.

Tony's favourite shift at Wadebridge was to book on at 9.0 am to work the Wenford branch. The locomotive would have been already prepared so within fifteen minutes they would be going 'off shed' to the goods yard to collect the train. Then came the run down to Boscarne and the 'interchange' sidings for the first shunting of the day, the clay wagons for the Western Region, destined for Lostwithiel and Fowey for shipment. Leaving Boscarne the train would proceed to Dunmere Wharf to shunt empties before running on to Pencarrow Wood to replenish the locomotive water tanks from the supply at Penhargard. This was a tricky operation on the return journey and required expert train handling. Water was critical as the tanks on the Beatties only

30587 gets some attention under the hoist at Wadebridge shed in May 1958. This is one of the three ancient 2-4-0 well tanks which survived at Wadebridge to work the Wenford branch. Final withdrawal would not occur for another four years and even then the old stalwarts managed a rail tour in London. R. Wilson, www.transporttreasury.co.uk

Adams O2 Class 0-4-4T on 3 September 1954 leaves Wadebridge with a train for Bodmin North. Photograph R.C. Riley, www.transporttreasury.co.uk

30586 on station pilot duties in June 1960. Photograph www.transporttreasury.co.uk

held 550 gallons. With a heavily loaded train of clay wagons (a full load was twenty wagons) on the return trip care had to be exercised so as not to overshoot the stopping place. To overshoot would be disastrous for with all of that weight it would be impossible to set back. The practice was to stop short of the column and then 'drift' in to the correct stopping point under very careful control. Skilful enginemanship, I'd reckon.

The 'water column' was a feature of the branch and by its very nature attracted photographers from far and wide. A water pipe had been tapped into spring water on the high ground above the line. This was then fed down to a gantry extended on iron brackets at above engine height to the lineside. From there a hand operated wheel valve and a short length of leather piping fed the water into the locomotive tank. Once replenished the train then proceeded on towards Helland Bridge and the wharves at Tresarrow siding, before eventually reaching Wenford. Another feature was the 'stop block' at Wenford which consisted of a wooden sleeper lashed to the rails. Most economical and how Southern, I had to point out.

The departure with a loaded train for Boscarne was timed for 4pm. At Boscarne the wagons for the Western were placed in the interchange siding, and the remainder in the goods yard at Wadebridge where they were collected by the 4.40pm 'through' goods service. The branch engine departed to shed. Just imagining the day, I can understand why for Tony it was a favourite!

The straggling nature of the Southern Railway in North Cornwall got it the name the 'Withered Arm'. It is clear why by looking at a map of the system, but though the service would be termed sparse by today's standards the Southern made the very best of what it had. After all much of it was single track and there was a limit to what could be worked, given the signalling and locomotives of the time. It is enough to note that entire holiday expresses were worked to the very farthest corners of Cornwall. It was quite something to leave your boarding house in Padstow or Bude after breakfast and be catching the Tube at Waterloo by teatime. The Southern men of all grades did excellently well on this difficult and demanding line which perhaps presented challenges (whisper it) which we did not encounter on our own Cornish double track main line.

Bodmin to Wadebridge and Padstow enjoyed a good passenger train service, and both had one goods train daily. There was also a regular service between Wadebridge and Launceston, Halwill, Okehampton and to Exeter. The North Cornwall Road, as they termed it, was a very testing line for the locomotives and those who crewed them. To the question, what was the preferred locomotives without hesitation the answer was the 'N' 2-6-0s, known as the 'Woolworths'. They were, above all, sufficiently powerful for their particular jobs and were reliable steamers with reserves of power if needed: 'they would go anywhere.' By contrast, the similar looking but three cylinder 'U1' 2-6-0s were not well

regarded. Wadebridge had two, 31900 and 31904; they had come from the flat country of Kent and, being made redundant elsewhere wasn't a ringing endorsement, exactly. The Wadebridge men were unused to their subtleties perhaps (if there were any) and they probably hadn't left the east in the best of nick. The inside cylinder and motion meant extra preparation work for no obvious benefit, so they were in bad odour all round, really. It was felt that they were suited to level stretches of track laid for fast running; there was little of that out of Wadebridge and the verdict is that they 'no good on the inclines'.

Wadebridge was at the very extremity of the system and the facilities, it might be expected, would not be extensive. Yet the reverse was true; in relative isolation the place had to be to an extent self sufficient and be able to keep its locos running through thick and thin. Exmouth Junction with all its workshops was just too far away. To 'keep the job going' at almost any cost was a point of honour at Wadebridge. They could lift locos off their axles and could carry out the fitting tasks as well as boiler work to a standard not enjoyed at many larger sheds. There was even an electric hoist on the coal stage to ease the work of coaling and we didn't have one of those even at Laira!

'I came off the road with a Beattie!' said Tony with something of the air of the confessional. I must have looked puzzled and, thinking that I had not heard him he repeated it again, with feeling as it were: *I came off the road with a Beattie!* 'So'. said I. And he told me. It transpired

Beattie well tanks 30585 and 30586 at Wadebridge in June 1962 with one of the new arrivals from Weymouth. R.C. Riley, www.transporttreasury.co.uk

T9 4-4-0 No.703 arrives at Wadebridge with the 10.40am train from Waterloo to Padstow in August 1939.

Western Region takeover at Wadebridge in July 1960. A 45XX tank waits to leave for Bodmin General whilst a pannier tank shunts some stock. Photograph R.C. Riley, transporttreasury.co.uk

that the track at the quay at Wadebridge was ancient, having been in place for a century perhaps and was moreover exceedingly 'tight' in its curvature. Probably when it had been laid the shunting was performed by horses, and they never derailed. On this occasion the driver misjudged the speed and the little Beattie promptly jumped the rails and sat on the cobbles, happy to stay there all day. This in fact was nothing out of the ordinary on the old quay line and its poor track as it happened, something to do with the springing and the bouncing gait of the 2-4-0Ts. Re-railing jacks and skids were summoned up and in no time at all things were back to normal.

With that my time was up, and Tony had to go outside and to assist with the other personnel in the re-ballasting of a section of track. When I think back to watching and listening to Tony, I can't help but notice that he spoke about the Southern with the same fondness and enthusiasm that I feel when talking about my own, proper railway. It is a depth of feeling common to many of the old steam men. They of course were just as proud of their railway as I was of mine. Which left me with a greater problem, *how the heck do I convert them?*

Another locomotive type associated with the North Cornwall line and Wadebridge shed was of course the T9 'Greyhound' 4-4-0. Although relatively late comers to the area, compared to the Beattie Well Tanks, they came to represent the very essence of motive power on the line. 30710, carrying the North Cornwall Line headcode, is parked at the rear of the shed in 1958 and would be withdrawn the following year.

A general view of Wadebridge (the shed roof and water tank rise beyond) on 3 September 1954. Wadebridge would lay dormant for a period to be suddenly thrust into life for twenty minutes or so. Three locos now go about their duties. To the left Beattie well tank 30586 shunts the goods shed while O2 0-4-4T 30203 is in the up loop on a Bodmin North train. Over on the right N 2-6-0 31848 takes coal in the shed yard. R.C. Riley, www.transporttreasury.co.uk

Beattie tank 30585 inside Wadebridge shed.

Though only three in number, the Wadebridge well tanks exhibited a number of detail differences. 30586 had for instance rectangular splashers for the leading coupled wheels and a panel extending forwards from the cab side sheet – contrast with 30585 above. Here it is outside the goods shed, the crew doubtless taking refreshment nearby. Photograph R. Ward, www.transporttreasury.co.uk

One of the three 1366 class outside cylinder pannier tanks drafted in by the Western Region, shunting the Wadebridge goods shed in time honoured fashion.

T9s and moguls (when Pacifics were present too the place entirely belied its remote branch line situation) occupy the shed yard in 1960...

30586 shunting Wadebridge goods yard in July 1960 with Driver Sid Ferrett and his nephew Fireman John Ferrett in charge. They pose with bowler hatted Inspector Smith who had travelled down from Exeter with the photographer Dick Riley on the footplate of a T9 4-4-0. They would later return with the same loco on the 'Padstow Perishables'. In BR days the division of duties for the three Beattie tanks was for one to work the Wenford Bridge line, another on shunting and piloting work, and the third spare. 30586 was normally confined to shunting and piloting work at Wadebridge as it had actually become unsuited for the Wenford line. In 1948 the water tank at Pencarrow Woods had been lowered and by misfortune 30586 had had its water filler raised, to prevent coal falling into the tank; it was thus only used on the branch in extremis. Photograph R.C. Riley, www.transporttreasury.co.uk

30583 (note the detail differences from above, including the lettering) at Wadebridge goods yard in June 1951. Photograph A. Scarsbrook, Initial Photographics.

RCTS Plymouth District rail tour, 5 May 1959. A four-car special Auto train was laid for enthusiasts from Paddington on the 'Brunel Centuria', with Plymouth members also involved, to celebrate the work of the great engineer. The four cars with pannier tank 6420 was is seen here on the 'Lipson curve' with Laira shed in the background. One of the new Type 4 D600 Warships is on the curve behind and another in the New Shed yard. P. Gray.

Chapter 10
Laira Engine Shed

The working of the engine shed (Motive Power Depot or MPD as British Railways termed it) at Laira was watched over and controlled by the most genial of persons, one by the name of Harold Luscombe. Known in Great Western days as the 'Head Foreman', he was to become a 'Shed Master' after nationalisation. Highly respected, Harold Luscombe was a railwayman through and through, who knew locomotives and how they worked from years of vast experience. By reason of this he 'ruled' the shed of the Kings, fairly but extremely firmly, prepared to listen but not to be swayed from what he knew to be right. He was supported in the day to day workings by shift foremen Harold Cook, later to become a footplate inspector, Vince Joiner, George Thomas, Fred Manley, Mark Peplar and Jack Chaston, a driver at Moorswater shed on the Looe line in an earlier life.

As a premier shed Laira covered locomotive workings of almost every description and was notable for its part in the working of all the expresses to London and other parts of the realm as well as innumerable stopping passenger trains. Amongst our most prestigious workings had been the ocean mail trains; trans-Atlantic liners called in at Plymouth Sound to offload passengers and bags of mail so they could be got to London a day or more earlier. There were local passenger trains and goods of every description on

the branches to Tavistock, Launceston and Yealmpton. The most notable of these was the comprehensive Plymouth-Saltash suburban service, a sophisticated operation of steam pull-push auto trains, with over 35 trains each day in both directions. The shed had a share in all the major freight services to and from Plymouth and there was an endless succession of trip and pick-up goods. Shunting turns abounded in yards and sidings in the city, including Plymouth Docks; the list was endless.

In addition to the above Laira supplied the locomotives for two little outstation sheds, at Princetown and Launceston. Two sets of men to cover early and late shifts were based at each shed and for many years Princetown on Dartmoor near the prison, with its line down to Yelverton, was home to the elegant little 44XX class 2-6-2Ts of even greater lineage than the much more numerous 45XX and 55XXs, which figure prominently in these pages. They actually appeared on the branch in its last years as the 44XX grew more old and frail. Laira also kept a venerable 21XX 0-6-0 pannier tank to which a 'V' blade snowplough would be fitted against the blizzards common on the Moor in the winter. Engines were stabled and serviced every evening on shed at Princetown but a changeover was effected at Yelverton every Monday by exchanging the 'old' one, in need of boiler washout, with a fresh one from Laira working a Plymouth-

Launceston train. There was a similar arrangement for Launceston, made by running the branch locomotive to Laira, normally with the up goods. The train returned behind a fresh locomotive for the next weeks work on the branch. The Plymouth to Launceston service was worked by our 45XX and 55XX small prairies and the crews stationed there shared the workings with Laira sets. Laira also worked trains from Plymouth to Tavistock, the main intermediate station on the way to Launceston and these at times were given over to pannier tanks.

****

In Chapter 3 I briefly mentioned meeting 90 year old Norman Williams at a retired members meeting at the GWRSA (GWR Staff Association) social club at Laira. He was a delight to talk to, and while he remembered, you were ever more aware of how sprightly and lively he was, especially so for his marvellous age; still enthusiastic with a winsome smile on his face as he talked. You could not help but notice that as each new thought came into his mind, he was seeing it and reliving every moment. You could not miss the passion with which he made his point, clearly echoing the love he had for the job. Born in Falmouth in Cornwall (he could do no wrong once I knew that) in 1920, the railway was in his blood, his father working in the parcels office at

Penzance station, and 6931 ALDBOROUGH HALL with 6.45 p.m. train for Plymouth, 17 August 1958. A.E. Bennett, www.transporttreasuy.co.uk

LAIRA ENGINE SHED 1933

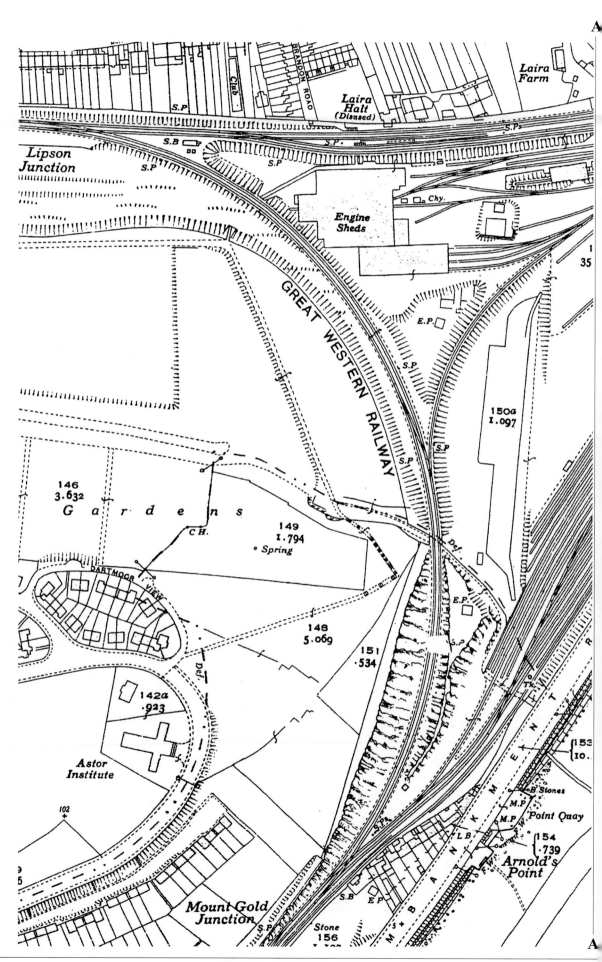

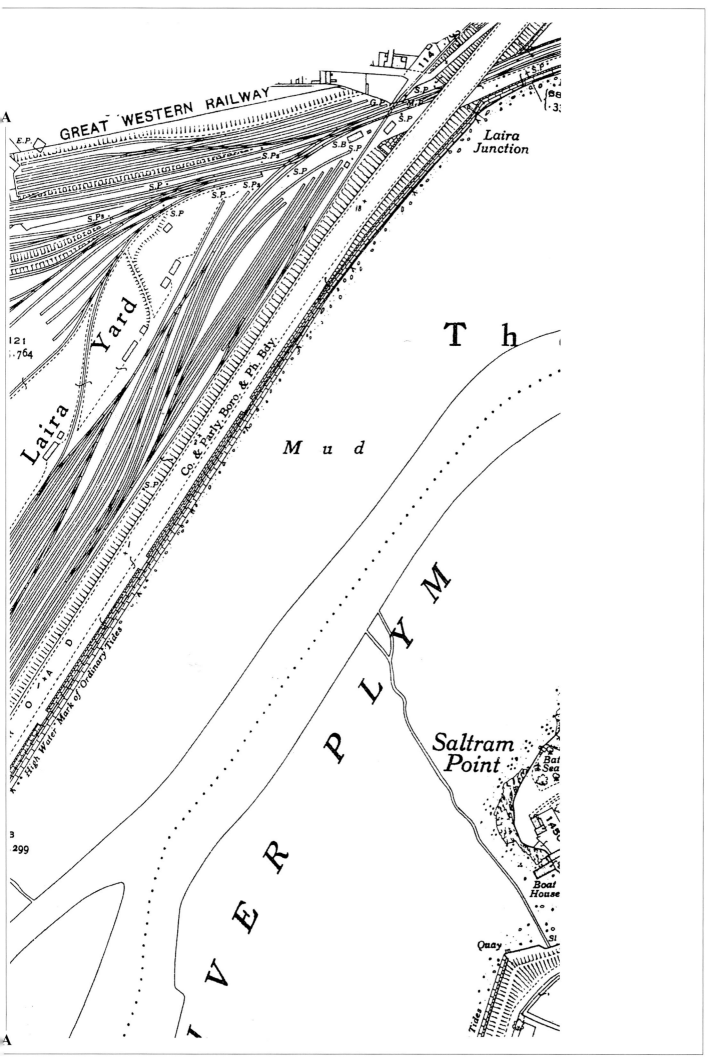

A

GREAT WESTERN RAILWAY

E.P.

S.P.

S.Ps.

S.P.

S.P.

S.P.

S.Ps.

S.P.

S.P.

S.P.

S.B S.P

S.P.

Laira Junction

121
.764

Laira Yard

Co. & Parly. Boro. & Ph. Bdy.

S.P.

M   u   d

T   h

P

L

Y

M

High Water Mark of Ordinary Tides

Saltram Point

Bat Sea

145

Boat House

R

I

V

E

R

Quay

St

299

Tides

A

141

Laira Junction Signal Box still controls the main line and the new road carries vehicles and their passengers to and from 'the Embankment' (Embankment Road) but off the beaten track and hidden from their view is a little bit of a former means of transport – the Lee Moor Tramway which finally officially closed in 1960. Its remnants still trundle up to its former crossing of the main line in June 1962. Contrast its ancient signal (still there by some miracle) with the harsh modernity on the main line beyond – the high lighting towers and vaulting concrete of the new Laira diesel depot.

Falmouth station. He left school at the age of 14, as all did then and went to work for a local builder to learn carpentry, though he was never offered an apprenticeship or indentures.

He did not take to the work and in 1936 went to the engine shed at Truro to ask for a job. Luckily there was a vacancy and he was taken on. Again with a smile on his face, he told me that his early duties, in addition to engine cleaning, was to light and tend the fires in the 'devils' by the water columns. The devil was a metal basket or drum, punched with holes like a garden incinerator, set on legs with a very high chimney. When the severe cold weather set in these devils would be placed beneath the arm of the water column and a fire lit in the drum. The heat of the smoke and fumes rising through the chimney was enough to stop the columns from freezing.

A fire also had to be lit in the pump house beneath Truro viaduct to protect the pipework during frost. The pump was a vital installation, for the water supply to the shed was dependent on it. In addition to this he also did his bit as call boy, waking up the crews in rotation and ensuring that they signed the register. When Norman was 'made' fireman he had to transfer to Swindon shed, but found life there very hard. A 16 year old lad away from home for the first time

and, being Cornish, he missed the sea and the sandy beaches; he enjoyed the outdoors, swimming every day in the summer, and now he could not even see the sea. It was also hard going on the money front.

Once lodgings and other essentials had been paid for, there was pitifully little left for any other needs. Taking a chance, Norman applied for a move to Laira and in 1939 his application proved successful and he returned to the West Country. He found more affordable lodgings in Laira, fairly close to the shed and was pleased to get a message from his family that dad had changed jobs. He was now a guard. What's more, he was moving up to Plymouth. By now, Norman was settling in at Laira, enjoying the range of duties and locomotives. He had also met a young lady, who would become his wife.

The years of daily routine work fade and merge in the mind but often odd episodes stand out. Such as the driver who grew his own tobacco. Quite how he accomplished this is far from clear – he'd have needed a greenhouse at the least – and some felony must have been involved, evading duty perhaps. Given that he had somehow overcome the barriers to bringing tobacco to maturity (the seeds would have come from a sailor contact) and that it would be pretty unsophisticated in terms of quality (no

A charming corner in June 1962, now sadly gone, lost beneath a roundabout. The Embankment bridge carries on over the Lee Moor Tramway curving away to the right; Laira diesel depot is behind us. The Laira Inn is fondly recalled by many former Laira men by its affectionate nickname, 'the Old Road'.

Finest Virginia, this) he was faced with the insurmountable problem of drying the leaves. Even the glorious summers of God's Own West Country might fall short in this regard but the 'baccy man', undeterred, had devised a technique for this, without having to pay for the heat. He simply brought the leaves in and strung them across the firebox backplate on a piece of string. I was left with the distinct feeling that there was more tobacco involved than he could possibly smoke himself and that a lucrative trade had been established. And all this in Plymouth, where His Majesty's Revenue officers were so alert to other forms of diverting that which was due the Crown!

Working his way up through the links, Norman eventually passed for driver and he stayed at Laira, on diesels and then the High Speed Trains (HSTs) until retirement in 1982. He has now been retired for more years, I suspect, than most of the people there have been working.

****

All the most interesting railway stories do not come from the footplate. A second nonagenarian at the Laira retired members section was one Leslie Crowther Haines, a one-time booking clerk at St Erth station; his father was the yard master at Laira yard, sandwiched between

the engine shed and Embankment Road. Before the Second World War, St Erth station had had a stationmaster, a Mr. Grenfell, a foreman and two clerks. Pay for a clerk pre-war was £55 a year and after paying for lodgings and other essentials of life left him barely enough to get home to Plymouth to see his parents. He was too young to merit any free passes to travel by train, so as in so much else we did then, he used his loaf. Knowing the guard of the train was central to success. He'd let him on (ten Woodbines always came in handy) to sit in his compartment out of sight.

One of the GWR's hotels lay on the headland at St Ives, the Tregenna Castle Hotel. Like all the company's hotels it was an exclusive establishment; 'high class' we called such a place then, while the less socially loaded term 'upmarket' would suffice now. It was patronised exclusively by people notable in society, even of international distinction. The German Ambassador to Great Britain, Joachim von Ribbentrop, later hanged after the Nuremburg tribunal, arrived at St Erth station by rail on his way to the hotel, as did Hele Selasse, King and Emperor of Ethiopia (Abyssinia). Such exalted persons could not be expected to arrive at St Ives behind a 45XX in the branch set, so instead were collected from St Erth station by a chauffeur-driven Rolls Royce, or possibly

a Mercedes Benz sent down from the German Embassy in Ribbentrop's case

Les also let me in to one of the secrets of why the farmland in that part of the county was so rich. The beaches had little seaweed left on them, as the farmers would regularly drive a horse and cart down, gather up the stuff which, it turns out, was a very rich fertiliser, and take it back to spread on the fields. Les could be a quiet, reserved person but he was passionate in his interests, particularly politics. His daughters, Mrs Susan (Sue) Orgill and Mrs Lesley Binney, to whom I am grateful for their help in compiling his story, laughed at that 'quiet and reserved'. They found him to be quite the opposite; to them their father was forceful and gregarious. I accept that when Les had a point to expound everyone listened, but he seldom spoke without giving a great deal of thought to what he wished to say. Having a firm belief in socialism (perhaps it was seeing the Nazi Ribbentrop in that limousine!) Les became one of the first Labour councillors on Devon County Council. He once presided at the reopening of a refurbished pub on the Plymouth to Plympton road. He enjoyed messing about in small boats on Plymouth Sound and this was only surpassed by a passion for jazz and traditional ale. I assume that before accepting the request to open the inn he

Laira Junction looking east on 29 August 1961, with a down freight (appropriately clay wagons) coming under the 'Embankment' on 29 August 1961, hauled by 2-6-2T 5569. Our pub, the 'Old Road' and the bit of tramway is at left – its forlorn signal can be seen there. The prairie tank is coming across the site of the tramway crossing. R.C. Riley, www.transporttreasury.co.uk

Plymouth Millbay looking towards the former station and offices (where I had my first interview for employment on the railway). The goods sidings are on the extreme right and the single line to the docks is sandwiched in between. R.C. Riley, www.transporttreasury.co.uk

first assured himself of the quality of the beer!

Les had a varied and most interesting railway career, eventually leaving Cornwall to become a clerk at the GWR's main office in Millbay, Plymouth, before progressing to a managerial position with the Southern Region at Plymouth Friary station. He was very much involved and concerned with matters of staff safety on the railway. He directed much of his attention to this field and his final position was safety officer based in the modern tower block at Plymouth North Road station, erected in the early 1960s. I have spoken with several railwaymen who recalled and paid tribute to his work in this regard and all confirm that little escaped his attention when it came to improving working practice. He had to investigate fatalities on the line and these could be very upsetting. A Laira driver of a diesel locomotive at the head of a train suddenly noticed a woman lying on the track some hundred yards off, awaiting death and was unable to stop in time – he'd have needed half a mile or so. This happened all the time on the railway and still does, more's the pity, but it affects men differently. Some can almost shrug it off, others can never come to terms with what has happened. The driver in this case was unable to cope, so much so that he suffered a breakdown

of his health from which he never recovered.

It was not until his funeral service that I found out Les had served in the Forces in the Second World War, attaining the rank of Lance Corporal early on, with the British Expeditionary Force in France. He was among the troops that found themselves cut off and left behind after the Dunkirk evacuation. Les found himself with RAF men and, it turned out, he was the highest ranking among them. Les led the group to a village on the coast, and 'liberated' a small fishing boat. Their boldness paid off for they crossed the English Channel safely and landed in England at Falmouth on the Cornish coast. It was enough to stifle any pangs of remorse for the lost livelihood of the hapless fishermen.

After reporting themselves present if not quite correct the group split up to go their separate ways, with Les catching the first available train home to Plymouth. Imagine the amazement and delight of his parents at his sudden appearance for their son had been posted 'missing, presumed dead'! Later he received a Mention in Despatches.

Les sadly died in September 2010. He was highly respected by all who became acquainted with him and will be very much missed, not only by his family, but also by the many retired members of the

Great Western Staff Association and the British Transport Pensioners Federation, whose meetings he regularly attended.

****

Sid Nosworthy started his career in conventional fashion, as an engine cleaner at Laira in 1942. The war meant a shortage of men and a consequent acceleration in promotions and he became a fireman after only a year, in 1943. Yet still, as convention demanded, he was posted away, to Oxford shed, as it turned out. Like nearly everyone else in his situation he immediately applied for a transfer home, and began to survey the vacancy lists daily. He returned to Laira in 1943, and eventually passed for driver.

He was an old hand on the double home lodging turns, and they could be wearisome for a family man. Nothing could halt the endless grinding wheel of the roster and the railway barely noticed Christmas. It is all very different now of course. The double home system made for a miserable Christmas Day, though you knew it was coming months in advance. One year Sid was booked 'double home' to London, not with an express passenger train, but of all things the up evening milk train for the depot at Kensington. The return was on Boxing Day with the milk empties. Old Oak Common hostel was unusually quiet, and

I am grateful to Plymouth photographer Peter Kerslake for sending this picture, prompted by my first book *Laira Fireman*. This shows a 'Boat Train' Special in 1954 running through the old Platform 6 road at North Road station hauled by 7036 TAUNTON CASTLE. A grimy 7905 FOWEY HALL stands in the siding adjacent to Platform 8 road – this had one of those impenetrable/amusing railway names but this time I fail the memory test, I'm afraid. Peter recalls: *These boat trains were difficult to capture on film, not being advertised in advance but when the signal shown in the shot for platform 6 came off well in advance it meant that something special was coming up from Millbay, booked non-stop and my luck was in that particular day. I was surprised to see it headed not by one of Laira's finest but Old Oak Common's 7036 – at least the Laira boys had done their best to put it out in presentable condition.*

The days of the Transfer Link – my old Driver, Tren Gil, and the 'Doublebois Goods' shunting at Liskeard. R.E. Vincent, www.transporttreasury.co.uk

there was nothing like the usual number of crews there. Old Oak shed itself was the same and little assistance was forthcoming in engine preparation. To this day he wonders if it was really necessary to have such a booked turn on the most 'family' day of the year, and that surely, if the train was that important, it could have been 'split' between various sheds. It's the little things...

****

At a talk to a group of enthusiasts at the Bere Ferrers station, on the old Southern line from Friary to Gunnislake a gentleman came to shake my hand and tell me: 'You knew my dad'. He turned out to be David Stanbury, son to Albert, once a driver at Laira. As I have already mentioned, it was Albert who was my driver on my very first trip to Newquay. I am sure that if anyone is reading this they will know that from that moment on, I was busy answering David's questions concerning my time with his father. For both of us it was a little of the past being brought to the fore. Bert, as Albert liked to be known, was a similar man in many ways to Claude Bolt, my driver in the No.2 Goods Link. He was a quiet and gentle man, for all of his imposing physical appearance; tall and well built, he was known for the interest he took in those young lads that fired to him. He encouraged them to have a 'feel' for the manner of the working of a steam locomotive, just as he had in his method of driving.

As young firemen we were expected to attend, when not on duty, what were known as 'Mutual Improvement Classes' usually held on Sunday mornings. The instruction was given by volunteer drivers, and delved into the intricate workings of a steam locomotive, as well as the requirements in the working of trains as contained in the Great Western Rule book; 'the Bible' as it was known. In my early days these classes were held in Millbay station, but when it closed down certain drivers, such as Bert, were generous enough to offer up their own homes for this purpose. David recalled as a young lad their home being filled on many a Sunday morning with a collection of fireman and even some young cleaners. We listened and learned and in theory were there of our own volition. Yet we were not really free to attend or not, for we were left in no doubt that, assuming we were not booked for a Sunday morning turn, we were expected to attend. My driver, Claude, was also an instructor as were others, and in all possibility was one of those who assisted Bert in teaching. No slide shows or computers; even ballpoint pens were at a premium, so the copious notes were made in pencil (short, stubby and 'found' somewhere) and entered into dog-eared notebooks with turned up corners. I cannot but feel that the main reason for attendance was tea and homemade cakes and sponges provided by Mrs. Stanbury! One of Bert's close friends was Driver Harry Roach and they enjoyed a mutual

respect and a kinship almost like that of brothers, close ones at that. Yet the love of these two men for their chosen way of life on the railway, and for the locomotives, nonetheless did not blind them to the grimmer realities of the new nationalised railway. By the late 1950s a steady decline in the standards they had grown up with in the job could not be ignored. So pessimistic were they about what the future held, feeling that it would offer nothing like the job satisfaction and security that actively discouraged their sons from following in their footsteps. David, Bert's son, was encouraged to train as a television engineer before joining the Royal Air Force in 1958, and his chum from Plympton Grammar School, Arthur Roach's son Harry, served an apprenticeship and moved to Australia to work as an engineer. Upon retirement Harry and his wife also moved to Australia to be united with son Arthur and his family.

****

T.W. Nicholls was our local railway photographer, one with more reasons for his hobby than most; if only for a short time he was a Laira man like the rest of us! Terry's first interest in all things trains came from his schooldays when, as a young 'spotter' living in the St Budeaux area of Plymouth, he would catch the Saltash Motor, nicknamed 'the stinker', at St Budeaux platform and ride, sometimes in the driving vestibule, across the Royal Albert Bridge to Saltash and back. The fare was 'tuppence', two old pennies. He spent most of his school holidays and free time at the lineside and formed a friendship with the signalmen at St Budeaux East box who, unofficially of course, invited him up where he could then 'spot' both the Great Western and Southern at the same time.

Unfortunately when he left school in 1957, a hearing defect did not allow him to follow his chosen path, the footplate and instead he tried for his second choice, a draughtsman in the WR Civil Engineers in Plymouth. This would meaning going to Swindon for a period so he declined but he was fortunate enough to be offered a position as a foremans clerk with the Carriage and Wagon Department at Plymouth Millbay. On the railway in those days, with the re-organisation of posts, Terry found himself transferred as a clerk at Laira shed, and it was there that I first met him. It was time of changeover from steam to diesels but, in his words 'Steam was for me the King and the Castle, and still some were left. I felt that everything was still regarded as Great Western'. Terry's career 'took off' from those days, with a promotion to the Divisional Offices in Bristol, transfer to Bath Road diesel depot and then to the Temple Meads Traction Control Centre. He was to meet the lady who became his wife in Bristol. She was the daughter of a Bath Road driver and they were to make their home at Bristol where Terry still lives.

For all of this successful career, and he has no regrets, he still recalls his time at Laira amongst the great steam locomotives of the day as among the happiest: 'Going to work was a pleasure. Most days would bring a humorous incident, and I have not laughed as much since!' Having lost contact when I left the Railway in 1962, I was fortunate to get in touch again when seeking his approval to use his images in *Laira Fireman*. Those of us with a love of the 'old railways and steam locomotives' owe a huge debt to the many railway photographers of those days. This devoted band, Terry included, have given me and others of us, no doubt, endless hours of pleasure just looking at their work and reflecting.

The engine shed at Laira was built in 1901 to relieve the old South Devon Railway shed at Millbay in Plymouth, where there was no room for expansion; with the growth of the railway in the West it was starting to 'bulge at the seams'. The new shed at Laira was built under Chief Engineer William Dean, Churchward's predecessor and was termed a 'Dean Roundhouse', something of a misnomer because it was a square building. The name derived from the turntable inside and the 24 engine stabling roads radiating out from it like the spokes of a wheel. Later, in 1931, a four road straight shed was erected alongside. This of course was immediately labelled the 'New Shed' while the roundhouse was forever after the 'Old Shed'. Laira me, being a contrary lot, usually called the new building simply the 'Long Shed'.

Allocation 1959

King 4-6-0: 6004 KING GEORGE III, 6007 KING WILLIAM III, 6010 KING CHARLES I, 6016 KING EDWARD V, 6021 KING RICHARD II, 6025 KING HENRY III, 6026 KING JOHN, 6027 KING RICHARD I, 6029 KING EDWARD VIII.

CASTLE 4-6-0: 4077 CHEPSTOW CASTLE, 4087 CARDIGAN CASTLE, 5021 WHITTINGTON CASTLE, 5028 LLANTILLO CASTLE, 5058 EARL OF CLANCARTY, 5069 ISAMBARD KINGDOM BRUNEL, 5075 WELLINGTON, 5098 CLIFFORD CASTLE, 7006 LYDFORD CASTLE, 7022 HEREFORD CASTLE, 7031 CROMWELL'S CASTLE

COUNTY 4-6-0: 1010 COUNTY OF CAERNARVON, 1015 COUNTY OF GLOUCESTER, 1021 COUNTY OF MONTGOMERY

HALL 4-6-0: 4928 GATACRE HALL, 5972 OLTON HALL, 6913 LEVENS HALL, 6921 BORWICK HALL, 6941 FILLONGLEY HALL, 6988 SWITHLAND HALL, 7905 FOWEY HALL

GRANGE 4-6-0: 6849 WALTON GRANGE, 6850 CLEEVE GRANGE, 6863 DOLHYWELL GRANGE, 6871 BURTON GRANGE, 6873 CARADOC GRANGE

MANOR 4-6-0: 7812 ERLESTOKE MANOR, 7813 FRESHFORD MANOR, 7820 DINMORE MANOR

47XX 2-8-0: 4705

28XX 2-8-0: 2809, 2843, 2899, 3862

43XX 2-6-0: 6301, 6319, 7333, 7335

51XX 2-6-2T: 5106, 5148, 5175

The mist hangs above the River Tamar on a September day in 1960, as Laira's 5098 CLIFFORD CASTLE takes her train out of Cornwall and back across the Royal Albert Bridge into Devon. Memories are made of this! R.C. Riley, www.transporttreasury.co.uk

Small prairie 5572 has arrived at Launceston with an afternoon passenger train, 21 October 1961. By the amount of steam coming from the area of the cab I would imagine that the fireman is busy 'cleaning up and damping down'. Driver 'Bunny' Amery has just filled the tanks and will be glad to get back on the footplate out of the wintry conditions. Terry Nicholls.

So they went and built a road bridge! But Brunel's masterpiece ignores the imposter. The DMU on 28 August 1961 is a poor sight compared to the 64XX Auto, but better this than no trains at all! R.C. Riley, www.transporttreasury.co.uk

45XX 2-6-2T: 4571, 4591, 4592, 5511, 5531, 5567, 5569, 5572
16XX 0-6-0PT: 1650
1361 0-6-0ST: 1361, 1363, 1364
14XX 0-4-2T: 1421, 1434
57XX 0-6-0PT: 3675, 3686, 3787,3790, 4658,4679, 9711, 9716
64XX 0-6-0PT: 6402, 6406, 6414, 6419, 6420, 6421
94XX 0-6-0PT: 8422, 9433, 9467

In my recollection, at least, the railway was a perfectly 'fair' employer, certainly by the lights of the time. Of course not always did it go smoothly, but overall managers and managed seemed to work together at least tolerably well. My sentiments are echoed by others among my former colleagues, though certainly not by all. Friend and former driver Len Hill, on reading *Laira Fireman* took me to task: 'But Phil, you have it wrong. It was an awful job. We sweated and shovelled coal and did our work in the most terrible conditions. And for what? For b——y awful poor pay!' Well, I accept that to a point, but no one said that the work would be easy and it was plenty hard enough for all working men anywhere, without the relative security of railway work. And it is true that the footplate and the engine shed was not your common or garden workplace; we chose to do this job, and many of us hated the notion of working indoors for hour after hour, day after day for ever. After leaving the railway, reluctantly, I indeed had a '8 to

5' job, with a hour for lunch, and I could spend much of my time in the open air, but there were times when I wondered 'what if?'

At times things were awkward, and differences between the two sides could not be resolved. Even families fall out from time to time after all. The railway was no different from any other large concern and sometimes passionate, even bitter disputes arose. Every shed had a representative body known as the Local District Committee, or LDC, appointed to act at local level where a grievance arose. In many cases these individuals did sterling work negotiating with the Shed Master or if necessary at Divisional level, and often succeeded in bringing about a result agreeable to both sides. During my career at Laira, such a person was Frank Thomas, who did a first rate job representing our interests. Latterly I have become aware of a second, Leonard Hill, who with a fellow representative Reg Green, gained a reputation as 'the best team ever'. In one instance during the changeover from steam to diesel, a time which provided fertile ground for dispute, a driver found that he had been taken off of his rostered duty which was with an early morning train to Penzance, for no apparent reason. This was typical fare. It was clearly a breach of agreed practice on the part of the roster clerk. Len duly approached the clerk who was adamant that the rosters stayed as published. Len had to go higher and he went to speak

with the Shed Master, and the reasons came to light. The return working for this job was to involve a new type of diesel loco and the driver had not been trained on the type. Now it might seem reasonable enough to the reader but our Len was having none of it. Agreed jobs came first and change had to be agreed. There were dark hints of industrial action. Typically, after the initial heat came the light of common sense. The driver left on his scheduled duty to Penzance and back. The return journey on the diesel saw him in his rightful place, the seat, but by his side was an instructor. Honour on both sides had eventually been preserved. A shame that it could not always happen like that.

Meetings of the Great Western Railway Staff Association Retired Members Section Meeting (wives are inclined to call it 'play school') always bring forth stories. Jim Mathews, a former driver asked me, had I ever heard the story of the 'Tregoss Moor fire'? Well, I expounded, moorland in a dry hot summer... by its nature, fires often break out. Mostly through the unthinking actions of a visitor, throwing away a cigarette end or discarding an empty glass bottle for the suns rays to play upon. At times moorland can even be deliberately burnt under strict control, as a means of management to get rid of unwanted undergrowth and to improve the quality of grazing. Jim patiently allowed me to demonstrate my arboricultural, or is it horticultural?

Mrs M Bayliss of Roche has sent in this picture of the ASLEF 1955 Strike Committee, St Blazey branch.

She says that most of the engine drivers pictured have now died, including her husband, W.G. Bayliss. During the strike, R. Squires, the treasurer, paid out 2/8d (old money) to each child.

Those pictured are: E. Dobson, G. Cowling, K. Hendry, A. Reid, R. Bartlett, S. Osbourne, R. Crossman, L. Hooper, W. Lawry, C. Stevens, W. G. Bayliss (branch secretary), G. Stephens, S. Bunt, and E. L. Bartlett.

No matter how good the relationship can be between employer and employee, at times it fractures and cannot be amicably resolved. Industrial Action results – observe these firebrands during the widespread ASLEF strike of 1955. The strike was widely adjudged misguided (it was about relative pay more than anything else) and accomplished little. It sadly laid the foundations for much lost traffic as the 1950s wore on. Mrs Bayliss/W.L. Rundle.

wisdom, before revealing that none of these circumstances was concerned; it was instead a good old fashioned lineside fire.

Jim was firing to Albert Nankivell in the mid-1950s on a rostered spare turn and they were delighted upon examining the duty sheet to see that an easy job beckoned the following day, for they were booked to pilot a special train for Royal Air Force personnel from Newquay. Examining the sheet further it was seen that the crew on the train engine was to be driver Charlie Cooke and his mate, whose name has escaped me. Booking on the next morning both sets found that they had been allocated a Castle, 7022 HEREFORD CASTLE for the train and 4087 CARDIGAN CASTLE as the pilot, or rather the 'assisting engine', at the front. Jim said that the 'prep' gang had done the outside, seen that all of the tools were present, checked the smokebox, trimmed the lamps and so on, and it was left to Jim to build up the fire and raise steam and to tidy up. Both engines were booked to go off shed 'coupled' and proceed to Millbay to collect the empty stock to work to Newquay, and to return with a train of RAF men

and equipment. Eventually arriving at Millbay, they coupled up to the train and the guard came to inform them that they had 'eleven on'. The run to Newquay was straightforward, and for two Castles with empty stock Luxulyan bank and the climb to Roche presented no difficulties.

Near Newquay the pilot came off at Tolcarn Junction, while 7022 took the stock on to the station, stopping short so as to be able to uncouple and run back towards Tolcarn. It appears that 4087 then shunted the carriages into an adjacent road ready for the passengers and their 'gear'. The two Castles then coupled together once more and ran to the junction, there to use the triangle to turn to face the right way, 'chimney first', for the journey.

Back on 4087, it seemed to Jim that they were a bit of a long way out of the platform, but he thought that it was just his imagination and said nothing to Albert his driver, who had already complained that progress seemed oddly sluggish. But then it was alright on the way down from Millbay so what could be the odds? They soon found out when the guard appeared, to announce that they now had a full load on, after acquiring more vehicles including

two vans loaded with personal gear and equipment. The grim-faced fireman on the train engine suggested adding a couple more and there would be no need to move for the engines would be in London and the guards brake still in Newquay! 'Right away' saw both Castles give that little sideways 'jig' on the rails before moving as happened with the GW locomotives when starting with a heavy load on the drawbar. The blast of the exhaust could have echoed at the other end of the county, at Lands End as the full weight started to move. By Quintrel Downs and St Columb Road they were aware that this train was to be no 'pushover', for it was 'hanging heavy' as we'd say. Facing the rising gradient at Tregoss Moor, hot ash was coming out of both chimneys; in Jim's words like fireworks on bonfire night. Was the loading figure they'd been given correct, had an error been made and they in fact overloaded, and if this was how it was on a comparatively easy gradient, what was it going to be like on Largin yet to come?

They reached Par in one piece and while waiting for a booked passenger train to clear it was made known to the footplate crews that their passage over the moor had not been without incident. They had set the whole of it alongside the track well and truly alight with the sparks and fire engines were arriving from all over Cornwall! 'All in a Days Work'.

The Cornubian: A Farewell to Steam in the West Country

On Sunday 3rd May 1964 the Exeter branch of the Railway Travel and Correspondence Society and The Plymouth Railway Circle hired an excursion train jointly, in order that steam enthusiasts from all over the country could mark the passing of steam. 'Cornubia' was the Roman name for the Celtic Kingdom which eventually became Cornwall. The excursion was to run Exeter-Plymouth and Plymouth-Penzance, returning to Plymouth and then Exeter.

Starting out at Exeter the locomotive was one of the few remaining 28XX 2-8-0s, 2887. High speed would not be in order for this trip and a maximum speed of 36 miles an hour going down Hemerdon Bank was considered quite creditable. The highlight was 2887 shunting its train back into Dainton tunnel in order to travel to Totnes on the wrong track, the down rails undergoing re-laying. There was an initial difficulty in obtaining reverse gear though a diesel was standing in the siding should it be needed. Thankfully this undesirable outcome was avoided, the driver eventually getting the reverse gear. The thirty or so photographers who had taken pictures of the train entering the tunnel

on the down line were able to run over the top of the tunnel quick enough to see the train emerging from the tunnel on the up line.

On arriving at Plymouth 2887 was replaced by a Southern West Country Pacific, 34002 SALISBURY. It would not merely mark the end of steam on the Cornish main line, but would be the last steam engine at Penzance. With the parlous state of WR express power by now it was, incidentally, the first SR Pacific to reach the terminus. The driver from Plymouth to Penzance and back was Albert Charles Stanbury, known inevitably as Bert, a top link Laira driver (he had also had the privilege of driving the last steam Royal train to Cornwall) in his last year before retirement and in his element back at the controls of such a wonderful steam locomotive. Until this time he had not driven a Southern Pacific but there was none of that inconvenient stuff about instruction! Steam was steam and he would get on with it. It was taking a bit of a chance actually, for certain characteristics of the loco and the techniques of handling were quite different from a Western 4-6-0. A Southern locomotive inspector was on the footplate, Mr L.F. Weaver who Bert considered 'a fine gentleman of which there are too few of these days'. SALISBURY was in original condition, beautifully clean and in excellent working order. Albert thought it 'a lovely engine' that he was both proud and pleased to have driven.

Local dignitaries including the Lord Mayor of Plymouth attended the train which finally left Plymouth North Road some fifteen minutes late. Nevertheless, Penzance was reached three minutes early, despite spending rather more than the allotted times at the intermediate stations. *The Western Evening Herald* noted that though the Cornish main line was 'no race track', SALISBURY 'responded brilliantly to the least touch on the controls, accelerated swiftly from stops and speed restrictions, and altogether was much more sprightly than the sorrowful note of the much-used whistle might have implied'. At Penzance, once the welcoming party, including once again the Mayor had completed their duties, the locomotive was uncoupled and reversed a mile or so to Long Rock, now the exclusive home of diesels, to make use of the turntable. It was a bit of a tight fit but 34002 in shining green was pretty as a picture steadily turning in the sunshine 'with a bright blue and white sea and St

Driver Albert Stanbury of Laira shed, in his last year prior to retirement, is on the footplate of SR West Country 34002 SALISBURY on 3 May 1964. The occasion was a special 'last steam train' organised by enthusiasts, and was to be the first occasion that a West Country had steamed to Penzance and back to Plymouth. The photograph was taken at Truro station down side, and the driver's hand is being shaken by the Mayor of Truro. David Stanbury.

Michael's Mount as a backcloth'. This was to be the last time that the venerable old Long Rock turntable was used for its intended purpose and it was removed and scrapped a little while later.

Departure from Penzance was witnessed by over 1,000 people on the platform, on the road or hanging from windows. The run back to Plymouth was 'an exhilarating journey over the Cornish switchback, with little knots of people at stations and individual photographers on the remotest embankment'. Arriving back at Plymouth North Road SALISBURY was replaced by 2887 for the slower paced return to Exeter.

Albert saw this memorable day as a fitting end to his life in the wonderful world of steam locomotive working. He appreciated the need for the diesels but felt that the new motive power, although efficient, lacked that sensation of a 'living thing' that most footplate men felt with steam. Although a forward thinking man, he nevertheless nurtured a strong nostalgia for the era of steam. He remembered his friends, and the locomotives with which he had worked, with a deep fondness and a great level of respect.

What better final image? On 3 May 1964 'The Last Steam Train to Leave Penzance Station' is driven by Bert Stanbury, to whom I had once fired. Fame by association! Thanks to David, his Son, for this memory of his Father. Hugh Ballantyne.

CONCLUSION

Writing two books has given me much pleasure as well as bringing back to mind the days long gone. In preparing this second book I have visited the Retired Members meetings at Plymouth Laira, St Blazey, St Austell, Truro and Redruth. I have received countless telephone calls and received letters from former men of the footplate and from enthusiasts. I have been privileged to talk to and meet with wives and widows, sons and daughters, and to listen to them tell of their husbands and fathers. I showed some of these letters and notes to my good friend and a former driver, Len Hill of Laira; I told him of a former cleaner boy at Laira who recalled with pleasure his first firing turn, with Len. That was the marvellous thing about working on the footplate, Len mused; it did not really end and here I was, back again after leaving the railway half a century before. A family we surely were.

In the South Porch of Ely Cathedral is a stone erected, I understand, in memory of two footplatemen, William Pickering and Richard Edger, killed in an accident on Christmas Eve 1845. The inscription reads:

The Spiritual Railway
The Line to Heaven by Christ was made
With Heavenly truth the Rails were Laid
From Earth to Heaven the Line extends
To Life Eternal where it ends
Repentance is the Station then
Where Passengers are taken in
No Fee for them is there to pay
For Jesus is Himself the way
Gods Word is Himself the first Engineer
It points the Way to Heaven so Dear
Through Tunnels dark and dreary here
It does the Way to Glory Steer
Gods Love the Fire, his Truth the Steam
Which drives the Engine and the Train
All You who would to Glory ride
Must come to Christ, In him Abide.
In First and Second and Third Class
Repentance, Faith and Holiness
You must the Way to Glory gain
Or You with Christ will not remain
Come then poor Sinner, now's the Time
At any Station or the Line
If you'll repent and turn from Sin
The Train will Stop and take You in!